CW00337550

26 -

THE AMERICAN DREAMS

THE REFLECTING SKIN
THE PASSION OF DARKLY NOON

two screenplays

Philip Ridley was born in the East End of London,
where he still lives and works. He studied painting at St
Martin's School of Art and has exhibited widely
throughout Europe. He has written three novels for adults
and six novels for children, including: *Krindlekrax*, winner
of the Smarties Prize for Children's Fiction and the W. H.
Smith Mind-Boggling Books Award; and *Kasper in the
Glitter*, shortlisted for the 1995 Whitbread Best Children's
Novel Award. His highly acclaimed screenplay for *The
Krays* (1990) – winner of the *Evening Standard* Best Film
of the Year Award – was soon followed by his debut
feature as both writer and director, *The Reflecting Skin*
(1990), which won eleven international awards, was voted
one of the Top Ten Films of the Year by the *Los Angeles
Times* and prompted *Rolling Stone* magazine to describe
him as 'a visionary'. In 1991 he was awarded the Most
Promising Newcomer to British Film at the *Evening
Standard* Film Awards. His second feature film *The
Passion of Darkly Noon* (1995), a cult classic, won the Best
Director Prize at the Fantasporto International Film
Festival. His first stage play, the award-winning *The
Pitchfork Disney*, was premiered at the Bush Theatre,
London, in 1991. His second stage play, *The Fastest Clock
in the Universe*, was premiered at the Hampstead Theatre,
London, in 1992 and won the Meyer-Whitworth Prize, a
Time Out Award, and both the Critics' Circle and the
Evening Standard Award for Most Promising Playwright –
the only time the *Evening Standard* has given the Most
Promising Award to the same person twice, for both film
and theatre. *Ghost from a Perfect Place*, his third stage
play, was premiered at the Hampstead Theatre in 1994.
His work has been translated into sixteen languages,
including Japanese.

by the same author

Plays
The Pitchfork Disney★
The Fastest Clock in the Universe★
Ghost from a Perfect Place★

Screenplays
The Krays★
The American Dreams: The Reflecting Skin *and*
The Passion of Darkly Noon★

Fiction
Crocodilia
In the Eyes of Mr Fury
Flamingoes in Orbit

For children
Mercedes Ice
Dakota of the White Flats
Krindlekrax
Meteorite Spoon
Kasper in the Glitter
Scribbleboy

For younger children
The Hooligan's Shampoo
Dreamboat Zing

★ *Published by Methuen*

THE AMERICAN DREAMS:

THE REFLECTING SKIN
THE PASSION OF DARKLY NOON

two screenplays by
Philip Ridley

Methuen Film

METHUEN SCREENPLAYS

Published by Methuen

The Reflecting Skin and *The Passion of Darkly Noon* copyright © 1997 by Philip Ridley
Introduction copyright © 1997 by Philip Ridley
Philip Ridley has asserted his right under the Copyright, Designs and Patents Act, 1988 to be identified as the author of this work.
'Look What You've Done (To My Skin)' (p. 118–22) and 'Who Will Love Me Now?' (p. 155–6) © 1997 by Philip Ridley
The Reflecting Skin stills photographer: Douglas Curran

First published in the United Kingdom in 1997 by Methuen,
Random House, 20 Vauxhall Bridge Road, London SW1V 2SA

Random House Australia (Pty) Limited
20 Alfred Street, Milsons Point, Sydney,
New South Wales 2061, Australia

Random House New Zealand Limited
18 Poland Road, Glenfield
Auckland 10, New Zealand

Random House South Africa (Pty) Limited
Endulini, 5A Jubilee Road, Parktown 2193, South Africa

Random House UK Limited Reg. No. 954009

A CIP catalogue record for this book
is available from the British Library

ISBN 0 413 71140 4

Typeset in 10 on 13.5 point Plantin Light
by Wilmaset Ltd, Birkenhead, Wirral
Printed and bound in Great Britain
by Cox & Wyman Ltd, Reading, Berkshire

CAUTION
This paperback edition is sold subject to the condition that it shall not, by way of trade or otherwise, be lent, resold, hired out, or otherwise circulated in any form of binding or cover other than that in which it is published and without a similar condition, including this condition, being imposed on the subsequent purchaser.

CONTENTS

Praise for **The Reflecting Skin:**

'*The Reflecting Skin* is an amazing film, studded with luminous performances and shot through with dark humour, that risks sheer over-the-top outrageousness at every turn but is so simultaneously inspired and controlled that it gets away with everything.' *Los Angeles Times*

'*The Reflecting Skin* combines the vividly imaginative, dark tension of Angela Carter or Dahl with the cruelty, bitterness and pain of Faulkner. It's ambitious, curious and unmistakeably a film no other English director could have made.' *NME*

'Ridley touches primal forces that most film-makers can't even imagine.' *LA Weekly*

'A hypnotic first feature ... Deservedly loaded with prizes ... a cult classic.' *Sight and Sound*

Praise for **The Passion of Darkly Noon:**

'So powerful is the spell it casts over the viewer that it feels as if some kind of alchemy is actually present *within* the film itself ... If only more British film-makers could conjure this degree of imaginative courage.' *ID Magazine*

'A slow-burning fable which builds inexorably towards a shocking climax that is part apocalyptic religious vision, part intellectual slasher movie ... the sparks really fly – literally and metaphorically – during the stunning twenty minute wrath of God finale.' *Time Out*

'Compelling ... the film positively soars.' *Sunday Times*

AUTHOR'S NOTE

FROM A RADIO INTERVIEW WITH PHILIP RIDLEY
TOKYO INTERNATIONAL FILM FESTIVAL 1996

Childhood is a big theme in your work. What was yours like?

I was born in the East End of London. All my family were
Eastenders. We all lived in the same two streets: grand-
parents, aunts, uncles, cousins, second-cousins. It was a real,
extended family. I think of my childhood as another planet
now.

What were you like on this planet?

What I'm like now really. I don't feel I've changed at all. For
as far back as I can remember all I've done is draw images
and write stories. I've still got fairy tales I wrote when I was
five years old. All I needed to keep me happy as a kid was a
pile of paper and a pencil. There's a photograph of me that
my Dad took when I was eighteen months old: I'm sitting up
in my high chair and I'm drawing. And – my God! – the
frown! The concentration. It's hard to believe.

Were your parents into the arts?

Well, both my parents were – still are – very good with their
hands. My Dad could – and still can – take a car apart and
put it back together again blindfold. My Mum trained as a
seamstress – she knitted all my jumpers and stuff when I was
a kid. And my Grandmother – she could knit the most

elaborate Fair Isle designs ... But 'the arts' as you mean it? No, that was anathema to them.

You must have scared them to death.

In many ways, I suppose I must. The things that interested me were so totally alien to them. For a start, they couldn't understand why a child would want to be alone so much of the time. I should be out playing with the crowd. But I've never felt part of the crowd. I've never really fitted in. The main thing that separated me as a child – apart from the fact that I wasn't interested in football: a capital offence in my street – was that, for the most part, I was very ill. I suffered from chronic asthma and was often bedridden for weeks. I was also given a drug called Etheldrene. It's banned now, so I've heard, because it's almost as strong an amphetamine as pure speed. So imagine the scene: an eight-year-old boy, obsessed with writing and drawing, confined to his room due to illness, and pumped up with enough speed to keep most teenagers raving for a week. No wonder I'd written countless novels and had my first exhibition by the age of fourteen. I was the original prescription drug junkie.

Were you a lonely child?

Not really. Or, if I was, I didn't recognise it. After all, I never knew any different. And the characters in my work were so real to me. They would keep me company. I used to talk to them as naturally as I'm talking to you. And – of course – there was reading.

What things did you read?

Comics at first. This was when I was about five or six. Things like Spiderman, Superman, Thor, Iron, Fantastic

Four, The X-Men – Oh, the X-Men were my favourite. I was obsessed with them. I used to write my own little stories about them, then enact them with the few friends I had.

What character were you?

Professor X. There was a paraplegic boy down our street and I'd use his wheelchair. It's terrible to think back on now: I used to whip him out of his chair, leave him crying and crawling on the pavement, then whizz off to become master of the X-Men.

Art has no mercy, eh?

No, *children* have no mercy. You know, the one thing that made me popular with other kids was my love of killing animals. Burning a spider with my magnifying glass was the one sure way of getting a crowd around me. Or chopping up worms. Or slowly crushing beetles. I was the High Executioner of Creepy Crawlies. I remember I wrote about it at school once. We were supposed to list our favourite things. So, along with writing, drawing, reading and the X-Men, I listed insect-torture and killing. My teacher was horrified. It was a good lesson to learn, though. There are certain truths people will *love* you for telling them, and certain truths people will *hate* you for telling them. And, I suppose, children pouring bleach on ladybirds is pretty high on the latter list.

There's a strong 'horror' element in nearly all your work.

After comics, the first novels I read were horror. And my favourite authors as a child and young teenager were all working in this genre.

Like who?

Oh, the list is endless. The first author I became obsessed with was Richard Matheson. I still think his *I am Legend* is one of the greatest novels ever written. Then there are the short stories of Robert Bloch – almost every one a masterpiece, I think. Oh, who else ... ? Philip K. Dick – probably my favourite writer. And Stephen King, of course. It's trendy to knock him at the moment, but *The Shining* is one of the few novels to scare me so much I had to sleep with the light on. Another one to do that was William Peter Blatty's, *The Exorcist*. In fact, I wrote a school essay about *The Exorcist* when I was fourteen years old.

What did the English teacher make of that?

Not much. I got a 'D'. His comment was along the lines of, 'A well-written piece about utter rubbish.' Another valuable lesson: people value subject matter above all else. Fluffy kittens playing in boots will always get a more favourable reaction than a twelve-year old girl masturbating with a crucifix.

Was this interest in horror reflected in your visual work as well?

Yes. Although I'm glad to say my Art teacher was a little more enlightened than my English. She commented on *how* I'd painted a severed head, not tell me I shouldn't be painting a severed head at all. Her name was Miss Driscoll and she was a big influence on me during my last year or so at school. She introduced me to artists like Bacon, Goya, Bosch, Dix, Dali, Beckmann, de Chirico – all of whom shared an interest in the darker side of human nature. I loved them all, especially de Chirico. And that's including the very late paintings, which people still take the piss out of.

The one thing Miss Driscoll frowned on me doing was constantly trying to get my friends to take their clothes off. I wanted to draw them in the nude, you see. More, I wanted to draw them with erections. And said as much.

How did they react?

The way most people still react: You pervert! You weirdo! But, for me, it seemed – and still seems – perfectly natural. But, you know, I'd been considered the school wierdo for so long that it hardly bothered me. My school mates thought everything about me was odd. My God – they even thought my taste in music was weird.

What was your taste in music?

Soundtracks. I was – I am – obsessed with film music. I would get – I *still* get – as excited about a new John Barry score as my friends would get over the new C.D. from their favourite band.

John Barry was the first film composer you got interested in?

Yes. And it wasn't the Bond music, although I think that's wonderful too. It was his score for *The Whisperers*. One of the loneliest pieces of music I've ever heard. And, of course, probably the greatest T.V. theme of all time: *The Persuaders*.

Who else do you like?

Oh ... as with horror writers, the list is endless. Bernard Herrmann, Jerry Goldsmith, Lalo Schifrin, Ennio Morricone, Ron Grainer, Jerry Fielding, John Williams. I've got all their soundtracks. I used to play this music to my friends. They would look at me like I belonged in a straightjacket. I remember once, at school, it became my turn to talk to morning assembly about a subject of my choice. Each pupil had to do this at least once. Most of my school mates talked about being kind to the elderly, or sporting heroes or – even more boring – Christianity. So I thought, fuck all that. I talked about John Barry and played his 'Capsule in Space' theme from *You Only Live Twice*.

And the reaction?

The pupils – well, they just sniggered. And the teachers – they pretty much dismissed it. But, then again, they were also dismissing my favourite classical composer. Shostakovitch. I told my Music teacher that I loved Shostakovitch's 'Symphony No. 5' and he said, 'I'll allow you Prokofiev, but never Shostakovitch.' Time, I think, has proved Mr Music Teacher wrong.

You don't have very many good things to say about your school years.

Oh, well ... there were good bits and bad bits, I suppose. And a few good teachers along the way. But, mainly, I was bored out of my skull. And nothing – absolutely nothing – I learnt there was of use later on. For the most part, I just did my own thing. State education is nothing more than legalised crime, as far as I'm concerned. We should be teaching children how to appreciate the colour yellow, not the fishing quota of Crewe in 1953. It doesn't matter how many facts you can spout about Shakespeare, if you can't cry at the end of *King Lear*. The Arts were virtually anathema at my school. You know, if I didn't want to do gym, I was sent to the library or Art Room *as punishment*. You get that? Art as punishment.

So I take it you weren't encouraged to go to art school?

No. But I didn't want or need their encouragement. I'd already got a fairly large portfolio of work – I'd been exhibiting since the age of fourteen. I'd already enrolled myself one day a week studying with the artist Cecil Collins. And I'd already decided I wanted to go to St Martin's School of Art.

You studied painting?

Yes. But, at art school, that's a pretty broad church. You could juggle with monkey heads and call it painting. Come to think of it, I think there were a few monkey-head jugglers in my year. As for me – I started my own theatre company: I wrote the plays, acted in them, composed the music and designed the sets. And – of course – I continued to explore my film-making.

Continued? You were making films before going to art school?

Long before. I'd always been interested in photography. As a child, my Grandmother let me use her old Box Brownie. I much preferred this to any of the new cameras. Its photos were always Dutch-angled and soft focus. Really dreamlike. And then, when I was about fourteen, I got a part time job and saved up for a Super 8 camera. And, by the time I went to St Martin's, I'd made one 16mm film and I was experimenting with video.

What were your student films like?

Mostly, they were my friends taking their clothes off and doing pornographic things.

Erections at last!

Hallelujah!

How did those pornographic student films lead to your first feature film?

Well, the student films – not all of them were pornographic, some of them were splatter – had got quite an underground following. I showed them at clubs. And there were tapes floating around. And one of the films came to the attention of British Screen and Channel Four, who were just starting their 'Short and Curlies' short films series. And I was asked if I wanted to write a ten-minute script. So I wrote *The Universe of Dermot Finn.*

This became quite a success, didn't it?

I suppose so. It was premiered at the Berlin Film Festival and received a standing ovation. The critics seemed to like it a hell of a lot. It was also released theatrically in the UK.

So how did the script for The Reflecting Skin *start to take shape?*

It came directly out of a sequence of drawings and paintings I did while still an art student called, 'American Gothic'. They were iconic images of America: children playing in wheatfields, black Cadillacs, clear blue skies behind Andrew Wyeth houses. A place where all the young men wore leather jackets and had jet black hair styled in quiffs, and all the women were blonde like Marilyn Monroe. But there was a darker element. When you looked closer at the children playing in the wheatfield, you realised they were torturing animals. The sexy young men with jackets and quiffs were holding Psycho knives.

You'd never been to America, though, had you?

That's the whole point. This was how I *imagined* America. You know, the American artist, Joseph Cornell, did it the other way round. He made little boxes full of the iconography of his imagined Europe. Images he'd taken from books and films and photographs. My America was exactly the same. It's how I *dreamed* America after years of reading American comics and horror novels. And, of course, seeing horror films.

You like horror films?

In my experience, most painters do.

Why is that?

Because painters see them purely as surrealism. A sequence of totally wonderful images. There's no moral dilemma or artistic snobbery. A good image is a good image. Horrific images should be judged like anything else: by colour, shape, composition. And, more importantly, what does it make you *feel*. Images are just unlockers of feeling, after all. And there's certainly a lot of unlocking in horror films. I'd rather see an exploding head than ... well, to be honest, I think I'd rather see an exploding head than just about anything.

So the images from your 'American Gothic' sequence became an idea for a film?

Gradually, yes. I invented a character to link them: a boy with dark hair and dressed vaguely 1950s called Seth – old

English for 'Devil'. So I did paintings called, '*Seth Plays with a Frog*' and another called, '*Seth Rides in a Cadillac*'. They were all beautiful on the surface, but riddled with menace on closer inspection. Is Seth playing with the frog or torturing it? Is Seth enjoying his ride in the Cadillac, or is he being driven to his murder? And, as I say, gradually I realised that all these images could be linked together to form a sort of mythical, hallucinogenic summer in the life of a child.

So you wrote it as a screenplay?

The original draft was called, *American Gothic*.

The film was, and still remains, one of the most audacious and bizarre debut features, especially from an English director. Didn't it worry you that you were biting off more than you could chew?

That was the main attraction. For me, at least. Others, of course, weren't so sure. A lot of people who knew my writing – but not my painting – couldn't understand why I'd want to shoot something set in America. After all, everything I'd written about up until then had been set in England: specifically the East End of London.

Your screenplay for The Krays *was going into production at about the same time, wasn't it?*

That's right. And you couldn't get a more typically East London project than that. I remember someone suggesting I re-set the story of *American Gothic* in England. I tried to explain that, firstly, *American Gothic* is not set in America, it's set in my mind. And, secondly, the imagery of the story wouldn't work anywhere else.

What's the English equivalent of a black Cadillac cruising through Idaho?

A Hillman Imp motoring through Suffolk.

Not quite the same.

Lacks a certain mythic quality, yes.

So off you went to America.

Well, Alberta in Canada, to be precise. By the time we came to shoot, that's the only place the wheat was unharvested. And by the time we started shooting, the film was now called *The Reflecting Skin*.

The film has a very distinctive look. How did you achieve that?

Well, I'd done a pretty detailed storyboard before we started. And this storyboard indicated, not only the various shots and their composition, but also the colour scheme that was to run through the film. The two colours that dominate the film are yellow and blue. The yellow, of course, is the wheat. Now wheat – even when it's at its ripest – is not yellow. It's a sort of dirty brown. So we used a range of coral filters on the camera to heighten the yellow. And, in some instances, I painted the wheat.

You painted the wheat?

The scene where Seth approaches Dolphin's house at the beginning of the film – all the wheat there is spray-painted Indian Yellow. Now when you mix that with the coral filters, plus the fact that we only shot during the late afternoon and magic hour, the effect is electrifying.

Explain more about the time you filmed.

I wanted to shoot when the sun was at its most intense and golden. And the shadows were longest. So we developed this routine. We'd arrive on location and rehearse for the morning. Everything would be worked out – performances, camera moves, everything – then we'd break for lunch, followed by one more quick rehearsal, then we'd shoot like fury between the hours of four and eight. It was a risky way of working – and I'm sure I gave my First Assistant several heart attacks – but it was worth it. Every morning we'd watch the rushes and the photography would, quite simply, take our breath away. Of course, I was working with Dick Pope who is one of the best in the business. He and I kept pushing the look of the film right through into post-production: we intensified the yellow yet again when grading the film at Technicolour.

And the second colour you mentioned, blue – that was the sky?

Yes.

And – against this blue and yellow – all the characters wear black?

Or grey. And sometimes, white. But never, *never* colour. I even got them to dye their hair. Both Viggo Mortensen and Jeremy Cooper – who played Cameron and Seth respectively – are blonde. But their hair was dyed blue-black for the film.

Jeremy Cooper's performance is quite remarkable. He doesn't act like a child usually does in a film.

That's what people found so disturbing. It's not an adult's *idea* of childhood. It's what childhood is *really* like. People have said to me, 'Oh, Seth is such a wicked, evil little boy.' And I always reply, 'No, he's not. He's just normal.' In many ways, you know, he is the only normal thing in the film.

Again, childhood is merciless?

Exactly. You know, anything with a kid in scares the shit out of me. *Mary Poppins* is a horror film in all but name, as far as I'm concerned. Replace Julie Andrews with Billie Whitelaw and you've got *The Omen*.

Did the child-actors understand the film?

When they were making it? No. They just had a good time. Their favourite plaything was the model of the dead baby – or Phoebe the Foetus, as they called it. But, afterwards, they all came to see the film when it was screened at the Vancouver Film Festival. And each of the three boys brought their school along. So the audience consisted of about four hundred ten-year-olds. And I tell you – they didn't stop laughing from beginning to end. The frog explodes – they howled! The father kills himself – they were on the floor! A kid is murdered – laugh, laugh! In a way, it was the best audience the film has ever had.

The kids got the black humour?

Absolutely. After all, when you tell most people the film's about paedophile-homosexual-child killers they don't usually get the funny side.

They didn't get the funny side when it was premiered at the Cannes Film Festival. Didn't half the audience storm out?

At the premiere, yes. The frog explodes over Lindsay

Duncan and – mass exodus. I attended that screening. I was so depressed I wanted to get on the first plane home. But, you know, a strange thing happened: that night everyone was talking about it. The press gave it lead reviews next morning. All the subsequent shows sold out. In fact, they had to hastily arrange extra screenings. I talked to a French journalist ten minutes after that first screening. He said to me, 'Your film is already a cult.' And he was right. It went on to become a huge festival hit.

But, with most people, I think it's fair to say that – as Derek Malcolm said in The Guardian *– 'It's a "love it or hate it" film.'*

To an extent I'm used to that. Everything I've done has received divided reactions. What surprised me with both *The Reflecting Skin* and, later, with *The Passion of Darkly Noon*, was the *intensity* of feeling. People either think the films are the best things they've ever seen, or they think they're over-the-top gobbledegook.

Some English critics were really outraged by just how, as they saw it, gratuitously over-the-top the films were.

Well, I'm outraged by most films' gratuitous understatement. Besides, *The Reflecting Skin* and *The Passion of Darkly Noon* are *about* being over-the-top. It's part of their language. Overstatement is just as much a weapon as understatement. Besides, overstatement – like beauty – is in the eyes of the beholder. Most people thought the exploding frog sequence not only over-the-top, but ugly. But, for me, it contains the most beautiful image in the film: Lindsay Duncan's blood splattered face against the sky. Porcelain white against blue. The jet black of the scarf and sunglasses. Barbaric, yes. But beautiful as well.

'Barbaric beauty'. This is the phrase I've read most often in connection with your work.

This 'barbaric beauty' thing has always been there. Even in my painting and drawing when I was at art school. For me, though, it's more to do with ... well, an hallucinogenic quality. Something intoxicating. Something that affects the senses. Like an acid trip. Particularly in these two films. Plot and character are the least of it. In fact, I always think if you see my films like acid trips you're half-way to understanding them. Forget logic, accept that anything can happen and usually does. Like a dream. Dreams are about images. We wake up, we remember images. Moments. Fleeting feelings. We don't remember the whole narrative. Don't be it, dream it.

Where did the idea for The Passion of Darkly Noon *come from?*

Directly out of shooting *The Reflecting Skin*. Every day, when we were on location, we had a two-hour drive from our hotel to the wheatfields. The journey took us past a religious cult commune. I never found out exactly what the cult was. But it was quite extreme. Very cut off. Barbed wire fence and everything. The whole Waco, Texas, scenario. Though by no means as big, of course. Anyway, every day we'd pass this thing and, mainly to amuse the children, I started to make up a story. About a young man who was born into a cult. A young man who has never seen the outside world. It was just playing around really. Improvising ... much like a touring pop group makes up songs in the bus.

And this young man was Darkly Noon?

That's the name I eventually gave him. Of course, lots of

things changed when I eventually wrote the script. But the main elements were there: Darkly's cult being attacked, Darkly surviving and roaming lost, Darkly eventually stumbling into a forest, Darkly being nursed back to health by a beautiful young woman. Right from the beginning it was like this. Very fable-like. A sort of horror-fairytale.

Many people have referred to your films as fairytales.

In many ways, they are. Some critics thought my screenplay to *The Krays* should be re-titled, *The Brothers Grimm*. And *The Reflecting Skin* is, amongst other things, a dark fairytale of childhood.

The Passion of Darkly Noon *is the most fairytale-like though, don't you agree?*

Without doubt. Don't forget – it started as a story for children, no matter how violent and sexual it became later. I've always thought of it as having a similar atmosphere to John Carpenter's, *The Fog*.

You like that film?

I think it is one of the most beautiful horror films I've seen. Along with Jack Clayton's *Turn of The Screw*.

Back to The Passion of Darkly Noon: *Say some more about the fairytale aspects.*

Well, its use of imagery is the most obvious. It's so deliberately simple: a handprint, a cave, a lake, a solitary house, and – of course – the most basic of all fairytale images: the dark forest. This stark simplicity also applies to the colour scheme: the symbolic uses of red and silver. We know instinctively what these colours represent, what they make us feel, because they have the simplicity of a fairytale. Red is ...?

Primal passion? Anger? Sex?

Silver is ...?

Enchantment? Love? Hope?

Exactly. You know, on one level, the whole film can be seen as the battle between red and silver.

Can you explain that?

I hope not.

The characters have this fairytale simplicity too, don't they?

Yes, yes. Darkly is the lost prince. Callie is the beautiful princess. Roxy is the witch in the woods. Jude is the court jester. Quincy is the prophetic wizard. Clay is the brooding knight. There's even a travelling band of players – the circus at the end.

But, in Darkly Noon, *it all gets horribly twisted.*

That's the whole point. The language of the fairytale – this simplicity of character and narrative – is, hopefully, just a framework on which to hang other ideas.

Some of these ideas are quite contentious. I'm thinking about Darkly's reaction to Callie.

Well, as I was telling this dark American fairytale – this fable about religion – it seemed to me I had to deal with one of most religions' deepest fears: women's sexuality. Their constant subjugation of women. Their age-old cry of calling any sexually threatening woman a witch.

As Darkly ends up calling Callie?

At the instigation of Roxy, yes. You see, that's what I was saying about the fairytale simplicity just being a framework. *Darkly Noon*, in many ways, is about 'the family'. The family as a destructive force.

The film's also about belief, though, surely?

That's the main thing, I guess. Darkly's dilemma is that he's in this place – this forest – without belief. Or, I should say, without his particular *brand* of belief. And, as the saying goes, when you take away someone's belief, they don't believe in nothing, they believe in anything. As Roxy says, 'It's like the Dark Ages.' A time of fractious cults, the wrath of God, apocalypse.

The whole film is just the journey towards this apocalyptic ending, isn't it?

That's right.

Some would say it's predictable.

Well, I hope they'd *all* say it's predictable. Because being predictable is the way such a film works. It's like *Carrie* or *The Shining*. The tension comes from waiting for the inevitable. It's the predictability of a bullfight: not *what's* going to happen, but *how* and *when*.

Well, for me, the how *is the most amazing thing. The end is so ... big.*

I always knew it had to be like that. Big! Loud! Over-the-top! It's about twenty minutes long. It took nearly three weeks to shoot. I was operating one of the cameras. Actors were standing in burning rooms. Hair was being singed. We all lost eyebrows. My cameraman, John de Borman, deserves a medal. In one day alone, we did nearly sixty different set-ups, which must be some kind of record. The final sequence has over five hundred cuts. Editing it was the closest I've come to painting in film. Leslie Healey, my editor, (and if there's a second medal, it should go to him) and I spent weeks cutting together yellow, followed by red, then orange, then a footstep, a scream, yellow, red, blue, red. It was the best time I had on the whole film. And – what's more to the point – it brings together all the main themes and images of the film.

Everyone's talking about the silver shoe here.

Each film I've done seems to have *one* scene that gets to people: with *The Krays* it was the sword in the mouth. With *The Reflecting Skin* it was the exploding frog. With *The Passion of Darkly Noon* it's –

The silver shoe?

The silver shoe.

So tell me more about it.

Well, there is actually a logic in how it came about. Not that logic is my main concern in what I do, I hasten to add. But, with the silver shoe, there happens to be one. I needed Darkly to see something that would send him on his path to madness. Something not of the forest. So I thought of the idea of having an object float down the river. That way it could be almost anything. All it had to seem was completely illogical and be a colour that Darkly hadn't seen in the woods before. Then, one day, I saw a television programme about how lots of small 'circus troops' – or freak shows – were appearing again all over America. So then I had it. A circus troop is wrecked in a storm downriver. Something from one of their acts is lost. Why not let them have a "The Giant's Shoe' exhibition – I've seen photographs of this kind of thing from the 1920s. So, hence ... the silver shoe.

But what does it mean?

Meaning is irrelevant. It's not a crossword puzzle. As I said before, it's what it makes you *feel* that's important. It's not intellectual, it's emotional. The meaning is the feeling. In lots of ways, my filmmaking is like the language of the pop song.

Can you explain that?

Well, if you dissect the individual elements in a pop song – if you get intellectual about it – then it rarely makes any sense. You can say, 'this lyric is nonsense' or 'why is the singer just howling and screaming here?' Or you can say, 'that chord is illogical.' And yet – when you put all these things together – BAHM! A song that tears your heart in two.

A big part of your particular 'BAHM' is the score.

Absolutely. In many ways, *Darkly Noon* is a lot like a dance. A tribal ballet. A lot of the music was written before I started filming. Locations, costumes, art direction ... everything was developed alongside the music. This is a very exciting way for me to work. Nick Bicât – the composer – and I discussed the script in great detail. The music grew along with my storyboard. And whenever music could tell the story, I let it. Again, for me, film is conveying feeling through images and music.

Nick Bicât, of course, worked on both films. As did the actor, Viggo Mortensen.

Viggo is one of the few people I've worked with who, I feel, is a true kindred spirit. From the moment we first met – when I was casting *The Reflecting Skin* in Los Angeles – it was as if we'd known each other all our lives. He understands my work totally. By the time we were doing *Darkly Noon* I hardly had to give him a word of direction. He knew instinctively what I wanted. Just as well really. Because Viggo – being Viggo – decided that, as he was playing a mute, he wouldn't speak at all for the duration of making the film.

Both The Reflecting Skin *and* The Passion of Darkly Noon *are regularly screened together at festivals now. You've given them the collective title* The American Dreams. *Was that always your intention?*

Yes. They're separate from the rest of my work. The only things, as I said, not set in the East End of London. They were always meant to form a different sequence.

They're very difficult films to categorise. They don't fit neatly into any one genre, do they?

Not at all. In video shops I've seen them shelved under everything imaginable. But, for me, if I had to put them under anything it'd be 'Science Fiction'.

Why?

Well ... it comes from another way I could describe the atmosphere of the films. It's inspired by some of those Philip K. Dick stories where, for half the novel, you think you're in an alternative history 1950s Los Angeles and then – WHAM! You realise that it's the year 2160 and you've been in the mind of someone in a coma, hallucinating what 1950s Los Angeles was like. It's the same with these two films. Imagine it's the year 2160 and a man is obsessed with what America is like in the past. He's also going through lots of emotional problems to do with religion, fear of illness, violence, suppressed sexuality. It's the custom of the day for a doctor to prescribe a special drug which will help this man with his various problems. The drug will make him have hallucinations so intense – a kind of virtual reality – that his psychosis will be exorcised. So the man takes this drug and, because of his obsession with America, he has ...

American Dreams?

Exactly. And everything the man has seen about America – black Cadillacs, Andrew Wyeth paintings, Stephen King books, the horror films of the 1970s and '80s – works its way into the hallucinations. He's even read American classics like *The Wizard of Oz* – And that works its way in too.

What bit of the novel?

The glittering, magic shoes that take Dorothy home, of course.

But the shoes are red, not silver.

Only in the film. The man has read the book. In the book, they're silver.

So ... when Darkly Noon sees the silver shoe for the first time, it's an image of – what? Yearning for home?

Perhaps.

And when he sees it for the second time, when it's burning, it's an image of – what? The possibility of returning home has gone?

Maybe.

So there's meaning after all?

What a scary thought.

For Viggo Mortensen –
who shares both the dreams

THE REFLECTING SKIN

'The whole of appearance is a toy.'

Wallace Stevens

CAST

SETH DOVE	Jeremy Cooper
CAMERON DOVE	Viggo Mortensen
DOLPHIN BLUE	Linsay Duncan
RUTH	Shiela Moore
LUKE	Duncan Fraser
KIM	Evan Hall
EBEN	Codie Lucas Wilbee
JOSHUA	David Longworth
SHERIFF TICKER	Robert Koons
DEPUTY	David Bloom
CASSIE	Sherry Bie
CADILLAC DRIVER	Jason Wolfe
CADILLAC PASSENGER	Dean Hass
CADILLAC PASSENGER	Guy Buller
CADILLAC PASSENGER	Jason Walker

Written and Directed by	Philip Ridley
Producers	Dominic Anciano
	Ray Burdis
Co-Producer	Di Roberts
Photographed by	Dick Pope
Music	Nick Bicât
Editor	Scott Thomas
Art Director	Rick Roberts
Wardrobe	Joanne Hansen

EXT. WHEATFIELD. DAY

Yellow!

A dazzling wheatfield.

We're high up, looking down, the entire frame full of this sunlit ...

Yellow! Yellow!

Then ...

A figure appears in the distance.

A shock of black amongst the gold.

Slowly – oh, so slowly – the figure walks towards us.

The camera begins to crane down ...

The sky is revealed: a flat, cloudless blue.

In the distance, a farmhouse gleams brilliant white and silver. The air shimmers with heat.

We're in the farmlands of Idaho. And – although we don't know it yet – it's the late 1950s.

Now we see –

The figure is a boy, about eight years old.

He is dressed in black trousers, dark grey, buttoned-up shirt: simple, plain and timeless.

His hair is as black as night;

He has a look somewhere between innocence and heartlessness – a bruised angel of a child.

His names is SETH.

SETH *gets closer, cutting his way through the sea of yellow.*

The camera cranes lower and lower ...

Now we see –

SETH *is holding the largest frog you've ever seen.*

It struggles and croaks but SETH*'s grip is tight, determined.*

As the camera reaches SETH*'s height ...*

3

SETH: Look at this wonderful frog!

Excited voices off camera. Children's voices.

SETH is grinning mischievously. He clutches the frog tighter as it struggles to escape. EBEN and KIM rush into shot, excited by the sight of the gigantic frog. EBEN is eight years old, dressed in simple, dark clothes. He has a round, cheerful face and wide, wondrous eyes. The kind of wonder that borders on dumb. KIM is dressed similarly to the other two boys, and he has a strange, genderless beauty. Of the three, SETH is the natural leader. There's something about him: his intensity, his darkness, his inexpressive cool that separates him. A detached gravity, at once both compelling and disturbing.

EBEN: Where d'ya get it?

SETH: Down by the river. It was just sitting on a log.

KIM: Look how big it is!

EBEN: Must be heavy.

SETH: Yeah! Come on.

They take the frog over to –

EXT. PATHWAY. DAY

– which runs alongside the wheatfield. It's dusty, bleached chalky-white by the heat. Long grass on either side, birds singing, insects droning.

SETH, KIM and EBEN kneel down in the middle of the path with the frog.

The pathway disappears over a ridge. SETH keeps an eye on this point – he's expecting someone . . .

SETH: Has she been by yet?

EBEN: No.

SETH: You sure?

KIM: Yeah.

SETH: You been watching?

4

KIM: Yeah. All the time! She's not been by.

SETH: Okay ... (*Indicating frog.*) Said I'd find a good one.

KIM (*feeling frog*): Look at its skin.

EBEN: Yeah!

SETH: She'll be coming any minute now. Let's hurry!

EBEN: My turn to blow!

KIM: Is not!

EBEN: Is too!

KIM: Is not!

SETH: Shut up! Who's got the reed? I'll blow!

> KIM *takes the reed from his pocket. It's about eleven inches long, hollowed out like a drinking straw. He handles it like something sacred, gives it to* SETH.

KIM: What can I do?

SETH: You can hold the frog.

EBEN: Well, I don't wanna just watch! I watched last time.

SETH: Shut up, Eben.

EBEN: Watching is nothing.

SETH: Just watch!

> EBEN *calms down –* SETH *is the kind of boy who demands obedience.*
>
> KIM *gets the frog into position, holding it with its backside towards* SETH. *Carefully,* SETH *inserts the straw into the frog's anus. The frog croaks painfully, causing the boys to giggle.* SETH *starts to blow through the end of the reed.*

EBEN: It's funny.

KIM: Yeah.

EBEN: Bet it hurts.

KIM (*giggling*): Yeah.

EBEN (*giggling*): Yeah.

> *We see the children's faces –*
>
> *The eyes bulging in horrific wonder as the frog (although we do not see it at this point) is being blown up like a balloon.*

5

Finally, SETH *is satisfied. He stops blowing, looks up and sees ...*

A dark figure is walking over the ridge.

SETH (*urgently*): Quick! She's coming!

SETH, EBEN *and* KIM *place the frog in the middle of the path, then hide amongst the long grass.*

The approaching figure is a woman. She is about forty, dressed entirely in black, with long, fair hair, clothes a little unkempt, dark glasses. We get the feeling that she's a beautiful woman who has let herself go.

There is a deep, self-conscious sorrow in her. It weighs her down – almost literally: She's walking slowly, every step an effort, full of operatic melancholy. Her name is DOLPHIN BLUE.

DOLPHIN *strolls down the path, lost in thought.*

A croak!

DOLPHIN *looks up. She sees the frog in the middle of the path. And now we see it too ... distorted, bloated to the size of a beach ball. Skin stretched so thin it's transparent.*

DOLPHIN *approaches the frog, attracted by magnetic disgust.* SETH *watches, fascinated.* KIM *and* EBEN *giggle with anticipation.* SETH *quietens them with an angry glare. Then ... he takes a home-made catapult from his pocket ...* KIM *and* EBEN *grin. Their excitement rises. They lick their lips.* SETH *loads the catapult with a pebble.*

Meanwhile, DOLPHIN *is staring at the grotesquely distended frog. She is right above it: half repulsed, half intrigued, completely curious.*

SETH *aims catapult at frog ...*

DOLPHIN *bends lower ...*

SETH *shoots catapult ...*

The pebble strikes the taut skin of the frog!

The frog explodes!

BANG!

Blood splatters DOLPHIN. *She screams.*

7

SETH, KIM *and* EBEN *erupt with laughter and run away* ... DOLPHIN, *dripping with blood, watches them* ... SETH *feels her stare. He slows, turns round.* SETH *looks at* DOLPHIN. DOLPHIN *stares at* SETH. *They're locked in this look for a beat* ... *then* SETH *dashes away with the others* ...

EXT. ABANDONED BARN. DAY
The landscape is vast, spacious, bathed in golden light.
   Long grass, endless wheatfields, insects buzzing.
   A small stream is in the foreground. In the distance, a huge, abandoned barn, like a dark, monstrous, skeleton.
   SETH, KIM *and* EBEN – *still giggling* – *rush into shot. They jump across the small stream and run towards the barn and* –

INT. THE BARN. DAY
– *enter.*
   Shafts of sunlight stab through cracks in the woodwork.
There are a few bales of straw, glinting gold.
   SETH, KIM *and* EBEN *sit breathless on the bales of straw.*

KIM: Ma says it's wicked.
SETH: What?
KIM: Exploding frogs.
SETH: Why?
KIM: She says it's a sin to kill things.
EBEN: It's just a frog.
KIM: Still says it's wrong. Bad to make it dead.
EBEN: My Ma's dead. She's in heaven.
KIM: No she's not! She's in a coffin!
EBEN: Not true. She's in heaven. She's an angel.
SETH: What's an angel?
KIM: A baby with wings. Every time you make your Ma cry you kill an angel.

SETH: I make my Ma cry all the time. Sometimes I just look at her and she cries.

EBEN: It's someone who doesn't blink. They go to heaven and become an angel.

KIM: That's not so, Eben. Look at your Ma. She's in a coffin being eaten by worms.

EBEN (*becoming tearful*): Not so.

KIM: You're going to cry, Eben.

EBEN: No.

SETH: Why your eyes wet then?

EBEN: No, they're not.

SETH: Yes they are! Go on! Cry for your dead Ma! Go on! Cry for your dead Ma! Go on! Cry for your dead Ma. She's dead, Eben.

KIM (*taking* SETH's *lead*): She's dead Eben!

SETH: She's dead Eben!

KIM: She's dead Eben.

> *Finally* EBEN *bursts into tears.* SETH *and* KIM *laugh out loud and start throwing straw at him, taunting him.*

SETH and KIM: Eben's crying! Eben's crying!

EBEN: Leave me alone.

SETH and KIM: Eben's crying!

> Eben's crying!
> Eben's crying!
> Eben's crying!

EXT. DOVE HOUSE/GARAGE. DAY

Both the house and the garage are very old, made of wood and in bad need of repair. The house, for its part, is two-storey, with porch. Unkempt grass grows all around.

The garage looks on the verge of collapsing. Even the sign, 'DOVE GARAGE' has letters missing. It now reads 'DOVE RAGE'.

The garage seems to be in the middle of a grassy wasteland.

Nothing in view for miles around. It's hard to imagine it doing much business. There's a watertank, a pile of old tyres and many, many rusting cars.

SETH *runs into shot.*

Passes the garage ... Toward the house ...

INT. DOVE HOUSE, KITCHEN. DAY

A woman, in her late forties, is swatting flies. Her hair tied in a bun, dress simple, colourless, functional. This is RUTH, SETH's *mother.*

The kitchen is simply furnished, poor-looking, everything faded: wooden table, sink, sofa – nothing decorated, nothing frivolous.

RUTH *is a stern, icy, woman, who moves with the nervous energy of a caged ferret.*

A man is sitting at the table, reading. He is balding, whiskered and frail: a milky ghost of a man. This is LUKE, SETH's *father.*

RUTH: Scrub all day and I can still smell it! Gasolene and grease!

RUTH *is obviously in the middle of berating* LUKE. *And she's enjoying every minute of it.* SETH *rushes in.* RUTH *glares at him momentarily, then continues with her tirade, undisturbed –*

RUTH (*at* LUKE): Your breath stinks of it! Your skin stinks of it!

SETH *sits at the table.* LUKE *glances at him and winks, playfully.* SETH *grins back.*

RUTH: I go to bed and the sheets stink of it. When neighbours call – not that they do call – I see them sniffing, sniffing ... (*Swats another fly.*) I spend all day bleaching the smell away, then you come home and I have to start all over again. There's not enough bleach to burn the stench of you away, Luke Dove ... (*Another fly.*) Your spit tastes of it, you know that? You're a walking time-bomb, Luke Dove. One day you'll sit in the sun and go up – BANG! You'll be – oh, what's the word? Incinerated! That's it! (*Another fly.*) Incinerated!

LUKE gives SETH another wink. Again, SETH winks back. Neither of them seem to take RUTH seriously; they've heard this a million times before. The repetition of her heartache has rendered it meaningless.

Now we can see what LUKE's reading: it's a cheap, pulp paperback, with a truly horrendous cover. Vampire Blood *is scrawled across it in Gothic lettering.*

RUTH: Well, it'll have to change when Cameron gets back. You hear me?

RUTH has gone over to a sideboard. There's an American flag on the wall behind. It is the backdrop for a framed photograph. The photograph is of a handsome, young man in a Marine uniform. This is CAMERON – SETH's older brother.

RUTH picks up the photo and stares at it adoringly.

RUTH: *He* won't want to be woken up by gasoline and grease. Not Cameron. He's been used to the pretty islands; pretty sea, pretty sand, everything pretty. Pretty islands where they've never heard of gasoline. Never thought of gasoline. Don't even *want* gasoline ... There's coconuts in the pretty islands. And not a car in sight. Just canoes. Not like this dump. Scrub all day and I can still smell it.

RUTH puts photograph back on sideboard, then sits at table with LUKE and SETH.

RUTH (*indicating LUKE*): He sweats gasoline, that man. It ... it oozes from him. That's the word. *Ooozes!* (*Slight pause.*) Ooooozzzzzzes!

RUTH looks at SETH and smiles – or the nearest her sour face can manage to a smile.

RUTH: Things will be different when Cameron gets back.
They'll change.

SETH: Think so, Ma?

RUTH: Oh, I know so.

SETH: I miss Cameron.

RUTH: I know, I know. I miss him too.

> RUTH *reaches out to touch* SETH's *hand. Instinctively, he pulls it away.*
>
> RUTH's *pent-up frustration — and now this rejection from her son — rises up, spills over into tears. She buries her face in her hands.* LUKE *rolls his eyes in irritation. There's no sympathy here — husband and wife are numb to each other's heartache. Its frequency has rendered it tasteless as water.*
>
> LUKE *gets up and walks out of the house.*
>
> SETH *follows and —*

EX. DOVE HOME/GARAGE. DAY

— hand in hand, they walk from house to garage.

LUKE: You thirsty, son?

SETH: No.

LUKE: Should drink. Turn to dust. Man's gotta drink.

SETH: You thirsty, Pa?

LUKE: I guess.

SETH: You want some water?

LUKE: That'll go down real nice, son.

> SETH *rushes off to water tank. He fills tin cup, then takes it to* LUKE, *who has settled on an old sofa on porch of garage to read his book.* SETH *gives water to* LUKE.

SETH: What you readin', Pa?

LUKE: Book.

SETH: What's it about?

LUKE: Vampires, son.

12

SETH: What's vampires?

LUKE: They're not very nice, son. They bite your neck and drink your blood. Stuff like that. Not very sociable.

SETH: What do they do that for, Pa?

LUKE: 'Cos if they don't, they get old. They do it to stay young. And then the person whose blood they drunk ... why, they get old. And then they die. And during the day they sleep in a coffin and at night they turn into a bat. If they feel so inclined.

SETH: Any vampires round these parts, Pa?

LUKE: Wouldn't be at all surprised.

SETH *sees something over* LUKE'S *shoulder ... it's* DOLPHIN BLUE.

SETH (*watching* DOLPHIN BLUE): You ever seen a vampire, Pa?

LUKE: No, son, I haven't. But, then again, I ain't been looking.

DOLPHIN *strides towards the house.* RUTH *comes out to meet her.*

SETH *stands up. He knows* DOLPHIN *has come to complain about the 'exploding frog' incident. He backs off the porch and, is just about to make a dash for it, when –*

A car pulls into the garage. It stops SETH *dead in his tracks. Because this is no ordinary car – at least, not for these parts. It's a Cadillac. It swerves into the garage, like a large, prowling animal, with skin made of sparkling black ice.*

SETH'S *eyes are wide with amazement. He's never seen anything like it.* LUKE, *for his part, is too immersed in his book to even look up.*

LUKE: See to it, Seth. My vampire's in convulsions.

SETH *goes over to the Cadillac. Four young men are inside. All these men are in their late-teens, early twenties and extremely good-looking. Their complexions are smooth. Their smiles, dazzling. Eyes twinkling. Hair, jet*

13

black and styled in a quiff. The DRIVER *of the Cadillac is the most enigmatic of them. His face has a merciless, perfect beauty, his voice dangerously seductive.*

The DRIVER *looks at* SETH *and grins.*

DRIVER: Fill her up.... Please.

SETH *does so. The* DRIVER *watches him in rear-view mirror.*

DRIVER: What's your name?

SETH: Seth.

DRIVER: Seth what?

SETH: Seth Dove.

DRIVER: How old are you, Seth Dove?

SETH: Nearly nine.

SETH *finishes filling the engine and returns to the* DRIVER's *window.*

DRIVER (*indicating* LUKE): That your father up there?

SETH: Yeah.

DRIVER: He looks like a scarecrow. Are you a scarecrow's son?

SETH: No.

DRIVER: I was hoping you were.

DRIVER *strokes* SETH's *cheek, runs his finger across the child's lips.* SETH *is transfixed, hypnotised.*

DRIVER: We'll be seeing you. Would you like that?

SETH: Yeah.

The car pulls away, spewing dust behind. SETH *watches it disappear.*

RUTH (*off*): Seth!

EXT. DOVE HOME, BACKYARD. DAY
RUTH *is glaring angrily at* SETH.

RUTH: You've been exploding frogs again.

SETH: No.

15

RUTH: I heard different.

SETH: She lied!

RUTH: Who lied?

SETH: The English lady!

RUTH: I can see through you to the garage beyond. You get round there and say you're sorry.

SETH: But, Ma –

RUTH (*yelling*): Now!

EXT. DOLPHIN BLUE'S HOUSE. DAY
Blue sky.

Yellow wheatfield.

And white ...

A white, wooden two-storey house.

In the middle of an endless, sea of yellow wheatfield.

With a flat, blue sky beyond.

There's an unreal, almost hallucinogenic intensity to every-thing: too blue, too yellow, house too isolated.

SETH *nervously approaches house. Steps up onto porch.*
Knocks on door.

A beat.

DOLPHIN *opens door and looks down at him. She's wearing a shimmering, grey satin dressing gown.*

DOLPHIN: Come in ...

　　SETH *hesitates.*

DOLPHIN (*with ironic smile*): I won't bite.

　　SETH *enters ...*

INT. DOLPHIN'S HOUSE, MAIN ROOM. DAY
The inside of the house is completely incongruous to its surroundings. It's full of old photographs, nick-nacks, orna-ments. Everything seems to be to do with the sea: shells, starfish, preserved piranha, shark jaws, even a large, though broken,

16

*harpoon. This incongruity is both enchanting and disturbing in
equal measure.*

SETH *looks around, bewildered and intrigued.* DOLPHIN
stands by the window.

DOLPHIN: Sit down.
> *Timorously,* SETH *sits. He stares up at* DOLPHIN,
> *waiting.*

DOLPHIN: Frogs! Who cares! It's my dress I was worried
about. Did far worse when I was a child. Goodness, yes.
We used to tie fireworks to cats' tails and set them on
fire. Ever done that?
> SETH *shakes his head.* DOLPHIN *sits opposite him,
> smiling.*

DOLPHIN: Oh ... you should do it! Boy, do they move.
Woosh! Straight down the street. Arses burnt to a
cinder. I remember once, I put my Mum's canary in the
oven. It went 'pop'. Exploded. Just like that frog come
to think of it.
> SETH, *relaxing a little now, has become intrigued by the
> harpoon. Its metal tip glints in the sunlight.* DOLPHIN
> *follows his gaze.*

DOLPHIN: Oh ... my husband's family used to be into
whaling. Before they became farmers.
> SETH *still stares at the harpoon.*

DOLPHIN: You like it?
> SETH *nods.*

DOLPHIN: Take it. Go on.
> SETH *picks up harpoon. He holds it like a priceless relic.
> Then* SETH *notices a photograph. It's a black and white
> wedding photograph: a younger* DOLPHIN *with a young
> man – painfully young.*

SETH: Who's that?
> DOLPHIN *follows his gaze.*

DOLPHIN: That's me.

17

SETH: No. The man.

DOLPHIN: That's my husband. His name was Adam. I met him in London. I married him and came here. We were happy for one week. And, one day, I went into the barn ... and there he was: Face bright red, tongue blue, eyes going pop. (*A beat.*) He'd hung himself, you see.

SETH *stares impassively. The stare gives* DOLPHIN *no choice but to talk* ...

DOLPHIN: He was very beautiful. His eyes were ... his hair ... his skin ... Oh, his skin! He used to hold me in his arms and sing to me ... 'You are my sunshine, my only sunshine, you make me happy when skies are grey' ... Well, now there's no sunshine in my life. I hate sunshine ... Sometimes terrible things happen quite naturally.

SETH *looks at the photograph again.*

SETH: You look different.

DOLPHIN: Oh ... well, he made me younger, I suppose. Without him I get older by the minute. Bits of me fall off. I get up in the morning and half of me stays in bed. Can't bring myself to look in mirrors anymore. Tell me ... how old do you think I am?

SETH: Fifty.

DOLPHIN: Fifty! Well, what a compliment. Oh, no, I'm older than that. I'm two hundred years old. Can't you see all my wrinkles and grey hair? Look.

SETH: Yeah.

DOLPHIN: You can?

SETH *nods. His heartlessly innocent honesty stuns* DOLPHIN *momentarily. It also hardens something in her. She gets a small box from a nearby cupboard.*

DOLPHIN: Come and sit down next to me.

SETH *doesn't move.*

DOLPHIN: Come on!

SETH, *still holding harpoon, sits next to her.*

18

DOLPHIN *opens box. It's full of old photos, and other memorabilia. She takes a tooth from the box. Holds it in front of* SETH's *face.*

DOLPHIN: Do you know what that is?

SETH: No.

DOLPHIN: It's one of my Adam's teeth.

She takes something else from the box. SETH *stares . . .*

DOLPHIN: This? You know what this is?

SETH: Hair.

DOLPHIN: That's right. My husband's hair. These are his reading glasses . . . This is his comb . . . You see, it's all that's left of him now. Just a box of bits and pieces. You fall in love. And, almost at once, that loved one dies. And you're left with nothing. Nothing at all. Just a few memories. And a house where he was a boy. Nothing but dreams and decay. And a box! A box from his childhood! A childhood you weren't even part of . . . Oh! *She has been rummaging in the box. A little bottle has spilled some of its contents. It's a bottle of Bay-Rum.*

DOLPHIN: Bay-Rum! Oh, this is the smell of him . . . *The Bay-Rum is on her fingers. She smells them . . . the grief erupts from her. She starts crying uncontrollably.*

DOLPHIN: Oh! It's him! It's the smell of him! The smell of him! Oh, my darling! My darling! . . . Smell my dead one!

DOLPHIN *holds out her hands towards* SETH.

SETH *jumps away.*

DOLPHIN *continues holding her hand out, weeping. She's a real evangelist in the sorrow department.*

DOLPHIN: Smell him!

Smell him!

Smell him!

SETH *runs from the house, and –*

EXT. DOLPHIN'S HOUSE. DAY
– *still clutching harpoon,* SETH *runs through wheat. He runs until –*

EXT. DOVE HOUSE. DAY
– *he runs up to porch.* SETH *leans harpoon against the wall. Then goes inside ...*

INT. DOVE HOUSE, SETH'S BEDROOM. NIGHT
SETH *is in his nightclothes now. He strikes a match and lights the bedside oil lamp.* SETH *settles into bed. He looks at the pulp novel we saw* LUKE *reading earlier.* SETH*'s eyes are full of fear.*

And now we see why ... On cover of the book is a painting of a woman; presumably the vampire of the title. And the woman looks remarkably like DOLPHIN BLUE.

SETH: A vampire ... ! She's a vampire!
> SETH *looks on the verge of panic for a second. Then, he calms and grabs his catapult ... he breaks the catapult into several pieces. Then – with the help of the rubber band – re-forms it into a crucifix.*

SETH: There!
> *Satisfied, he puts the crucifix under his pillow. He's about to look at the cover of the book again when –*
> *The door opens!*
> RUTH *steps into the room, eyes flaring.*

RUTH: You awake?
SETH: ... A little.
RUTH: Well, it's time you were asleep.
> RUTH *goes to blow the bedside lamp off.*

SETH: No, Ma!
RUTH: What is it now?
SETH: ... Nothing.

21

RUTH: Just grow up and go to sleep.

SETH: But –

RUTH: Do you want the water?

SETH: No.

RUTH: Then the light goes out.

    RUTH *blows lamp out and leaves. Instantly,* SETH *strikes the match to re-light it, but –*

        The door opens again. It's RUTH.

RUTH: Water!

INT. DOVE HOUSE, KITCHEN. NIGHT

SETH *is sitting at kitchen table, drinking a cup of water.* RUTH *is standing beside him with a large pitcher, waiting to re-fill the cup. There is water splashed over the table and down* SETH's *front – this is obviously not the first cup he's drunk since he's been there.*

    SETH *gasps, trying to drink –*

RUTH: Every last drop!

    SETH *puts cup down, spluttering.*

SETH: I can't! No more!

RUTH: You're not finished yet, my boy.

SETH: I'm gonna burst! I've got to go!

    RUTH *slaps* SETH *around the head. He cries out in pain.*

    RUTH *pours more water into the mug.*

RUTH: Not until you've finished. Every last drop. Go on! Drink.

SETH: I'll be sick.

RUTH: Then you'll just have to be sick. Keep on drinking.

    SETH *is nearly choking now.*

SETH: I can't, Ma. Really.

RUTH: Go on! You haven't finished.

SETH: Ma –

22

RUTH: Drink it! Drink it! Drink it!

RUTH snatches the cup from SETH. She pulls his head back. Pinches his nose. Pours the water down his throat. SETH is gagging, struggling. But RUTH is stronger.

RUTH: You gonna drink until your stomach's fit to burst. You're gonna drink it all, Seth Dove. Even if it takes you all night. You're gonna drink it all – (*Suddenly looks up, sniffing.*) I can smell your Father.

The door opens. LUKE enters, followed by JOSHUA. JOSHUA is in his late forties, dressed in severe black, with a look that screams 'religious maniac'. He is EBEN's father.

JOSHUA: The Lord's taken him because I'm a sinner. Just like he took my Rachel.

LUKE shoots RUTH a warning look, then sits on sofa. JOSHUA sits beside him.

RUTH: Taken who, Joshua?

JOSHUA: I am a sinner! I drink! I have bad thoughts.

RUTH: Somebody mind telling me what's going on?

LUKE: Eben's missing.

JOSHUA: We need the Sheriff. I keep telling him we should get the Sheriff Ticker.

RUTH and LUKE exchange nervous glances at the mention of TICKER's name.

RUTH: No need for Sheriff Ticker yet, Joshua.

LUKE: No, that's what I say. We're not sure anything's happened yet.

RUTH: 'Course we're not.

LUKE motions for SETH to come to him. SETH does so.

LUKE: When did you last see Eben, son?

SETH: This morning.

LUKE: Where did you leave him?

SETH is just about to answer when JOSHUA grabs him.

JOSHUA: Did the Lord take him, boy?

> SETH *struggles to get free. He's clutching at his stomach,*
> *obviously in pain.*

JOSHUA: Did the angels come down and pluck him from the
wheat? Did the Lord say, 'His Pa is a sinner and not
meant to be happy'?

SETH: No.

> SETH's *struggling increases. There's sweat on his face. The*
> *pain in his stomach causes him more and more distress.*

JOSHUA: Where was he going to, boy?

SETH: I've got to go! Pa!

> SETH *pisses over* JOSHUA.

INT. THE BARN. DAY

SETH *and* KIM *are throwing pebbles at a cow's skull.*

SETH: She's a vampire. She drinks blood to make her young.
She's afraid to look into mirrors in case her reflection is
gone. And she hates sunlight. And she keeps her
husband in a black box and his sweat in a bottle.

KIM: How do you know?

SETH: She told me. To my face. She's two hundred years
old.

KIM: No!

SETH: True!

KIM: Do you think she killed Eben?

SETH: Could be.

KIM: But ... why?

SETH: For his blood, stupid.

KIM: His *blood*?

SETH: Sure! If she don't get blood she starts to fall apart.
She said, 'I get up in the morning and there's my skin
left in the bed' ... Come on.

> SETH *stands and starts leaving.*

24

KIM: Where you going?

SETH (*firmly*): Just come on.

EXT. DOLPHIN'S HOUSE. DAY

Again ...

  Yellow wheat.

  Blue sky.

  White house.

  DOLPHIN *comes out of the house. She walks down path and out of shot.*

  SETH *and* KIM *stand up – they'd been hiding in the wheat, completely concealed by the ocean of gold. They rush over to the house, go to a side window, struggle with it. Finally, it opens and the two boys climb inside –*

INT. DOLPHIN'S HOUSE, MAIN ROOM. DAY

SETH *starts looking around.* KIM *watches.*

KIM: What are you looking for?

SETH: Her coffin.

KIM: Her coffin?

SETH: It's been here somewhere. She sleeps in it.

  KIM *looks upstairs.*

KIM: Let's go to her bedroom then.

SETH: Shall we?

KIM: Yes!

  SETH *and* KIM *rush upstairs and –*

INT. DOLPHIN'S HOUSE, BEDROOM. DAY

– in the middle of the room is a four-poster bed. Like downstairs, there are many nick-nacks from the sea. One is a very large shell that immediately captures SETH's *attention.*

26

SETH: Look at this wonderful shell.

KIM: Look how big it is!

They look in awe at the shell. Then ...

SETH (*gleefully*): I know! Let's smash it!

KIM: Yeah!

SETH *throws the shell across the room.* KIM, *not wanting to be left out, picks up a glass ornament and throws it. It shatters.*

SETH: Smash it!

KIM: Yeah!

SETH: Smash everything! Smash everything! Smash everything!

SETH *picks more things up and breaks them.*

KIM *follows suit.*

They are both squealing with delight.

Smash! Crash!

Whatever can be broken is broken.

Whatever can be smashed, is smashed.

Whatever torn, torn.

The boys are caught in an almost rabid frenzy now.

Crash!

Smash!

Tear!

They rip the sheets from the bed ...

SETH: Smash it!

KIM: Rip it!

SETH: Tear it!

KIM: Break it!

SETH: Smash everything!

KIM: Rip everything!

SETH: Tear everything!

KIM: Break everything!

They destroy things until they are too exhausted to do it anymore. They collapse to the bed, breathless. Then ...

They hear the front door open downstairs —

KIM (*suddenly alarmed*): She's back.

SETH: Shhh!

    SETH *and* KIM *jump up and* –

INT. DOLPHIN'S HOUSE, STAIRS/MAIN ROOM. DAY

– creep out of the bedroom. They peer through the bannisters into the main room downstairs.

    DOLPHIN *is sitting in a chair. Then, slowly,* DOLPHIN *starts to feel between her breasts. She moans a little.* KIM *nudges* SETH *and frowns: 'What's going on?'* SETH *merely shrugs: 'No idea!'* DOLPHIN *is feeling between her legs now. Her lips are trembling. A strange whimpering sound can be heard at the back of her throat.* SETH *and* KIM *are getting a little unsettled. They've never seen anything like this before.* DOLPHIN *starts to cry out, her hand working frantically now.*

    SETH *nudges* KIM *and indicates they should go downstairs. Try to get out. They do so ... making for the window through which they came.* DOLPHIN*'s cries are getting louder!* SETH *and* KIM *reach the window. They try to open it.* DOLPHIN, *who has her back to them, continues to bring herself to a climax.*

    Suddenly – the window makes a noise. DOLPHIN *jumps to her feet. She stares at* SETH *and* KIM. SETH *and* KIM *stare at her.*

    A frozen beat.

    Then ... DOLPHIN *screams!*

    SETH *and* KIM *scream!*

    DOLPHIN *screams louder!*

    SETH *and* KIM *scream louder. Then make a dash for the door.*

    DOLPHIN *continues to scream!*

    SETH *and* KIM *scamper out of the house and* –

EXT. DOLPHIN'S HOUSE, WHEATFIELD. DAY

– *rush away from the house, across a road and into the wheatfield opposite.*

SETH *stops and looks back.* DOLPHIN *has come out onto the porch to stare after them.* KIM, *in panic, keeps running out of shot.*

SETH *and* DOLPHIN *stare at each other.*

Then ... the sound of a car engine!

SETH *looks and sees the Cadillac parked nearby. It starts up and drives past the house and out of shot ...*

SETH *watches it disappear like a black shark through an ocean of yellow, intent on a kill.*

SETH *looks back at* DOLPHIN. DOLPHIN *goes back into house.*

Everything is still now.

Blue.

Yellow.

White ...

EXT. DOVE GARAGE. DAY

LUKE *is sitting on porch, reading a book.* SETH *steps up onto porch ...*

SETH: Hi, Pa.

LUKE: You thirsty, son?

SETH: No.

LUKE: You been running?

SETH: A little.

LUKE: Turn to dust. A man's gotta drink.

SETH: You thirsty, Pa?

LUKE: A little, son.

> SETH *goes to water tank. He picks up tin cup. He opens water tank. And –*
>
> *He stares in horror! Drops the cup.*

The dead body of EBEN *is floating in the tank. He is naked and bloated, white as snow.*

SETH: Pa!

LUKE: Mmm?

SETH: PA!

INT. DOVE HOUSE, KITCHEN. DAY

RUTH, LUKE *and* SETH *are sitting on the sofa.* RUTH *is tense, clutching a handkerchief, her eyes are bright red. But, if she's been crying, it's more with anger than sorrow.* LUKE *looks numb, expressionless. He is drained with shock.*

Sitting in a highback chair, and facing them, is a hard-faced man in his mid-twenties. This is the DEPUTY. *He's glaring at* LUKE *suspiciously, obviously in the middle of some sort of interrogation.*

In the background, we see the table set for dinner. Plates of food are getting cold.

DEPUTY: Now let's go over this again, shall we?

RUTH *rips her handkerchief in two, near hysteria with nerves.*

RUTH: How many times can he answer the same questions. He's told you all he knows.

DEPUTY: I think *I* should be the judge of that, don't you, ma'am. Unless, of course, there's a reason why you don't *want* me to ask questions?

RUTH: Reason? What do you mean? Why should I have a reason?

DEPUTY *shoots* LUKE *a look.*

DEPUTY: Had Sheriff Ticker on the phone.

RUTH (*anxiously*): Sheriff Ticker –

DEPUTY: You know Sheriff Ticker?

RUTH: Well ... I ... yes, I know him.

30

DEPUTY: He certainly seems to know your husband. Knows him real well. Has quite a lot to say about him, does Sheriff Ticker.

LUKE *is visibly blanching.* RUTH *is looking more and more nervous.*

RUTH: Go upstairs, Seth.

SETH: But, Ma –

RUTH: Do as you're told.

SETH: Ma!

RUTH: Go!

SETH *leaves the kitchen, but merely hides by the stairs, listening eagerly.*

A beat.

RUTH: What has Sheriff Ticker told you?

DEPUTY: You know full well what he's told us.

RUTH: It was years ago for the love of God. You gonna drag it up all over again?

DEPUTY: Might be it needs dragging up.

LUKE *is sobbing now. He buries his face in his hands.*

RUTH: Shut up! You'll only make it worse!

DEPUTY: He even cries like a woman.

RUTH: Don't you call my husband –

DEPUTY: In full embrace the Sheriff said. In the barn. Kissing the boy –

RUTH: He wasn't a boy. He was seventeen. And it was years ago –

DEPUTY: Sheriff Ticker said he felt sick. Two men. Kissing ... that's why you married him so quick. Protect his good name.

RUTH: Why don't you ask the Sheriff? He seems to know everything else.

DEPUTY: Oh, he does. He does know everything. And what he doesn't know ... he suspects. (*Glares at* LUKE.) This time you won't get away with it.

31

LUKE (*sobbing*): I didn't do ... I wouldn't hurt ... a child ...
   I wouldn't –

DEPUTY: I'd arrest you this very minute if I could –

RUTH: Arrest him for what? He hasn't done anything!

DEPUTY: Well, now, we can't be sure of that, can we?
   Sheriff Ticker says it's a short leap from kissing to
   killing.

   DEPUTY *strolls to the door, opens it, then glances back.*

DEPUTY: 'Bye now. Enjoy your supper.

   DEPUTY *leaves, chuckling.*

   RUTH *stands, ripping her handkerchief to shreds, eyes
   glaring.* LUKE *is whimpering on the sofa.* SETH *is listening
   from his hiding place, intrigued, horrified, fascinated.*

   Suddenly, RUTH *glares at* LUKE.

RUTH: Shut up! Shut up! (*Slaps* LUKE *violently.*) All that
   gossip! I can't go through it again. You hear me? I can't
   go through it again. I won't! Not for you! I won't! I
   won't!

   RUTH *calms down a little and sits down, exhausted by
   grief.*

RUTH: No, not for you.

   Slowly, LUKE *stops crying. His face becomes harder,
   determined. He's made his mind up about something. In
   one sudden movement, he jumps to his feet and leaves the
   house.*

RUTH: You come back here, Luke Dove!

   SETH *rushes out of the house –*

EXT. DOVE HOUSE/GARAGE. EVENING

– *following his Pa.* LUKE *walks – staggers – towards the
garage.*

   SETH *follows at a distance: still intrigued, still fascinated.
   It is a beautiful twilight.*

   Sky streaked with yellow and orange.

32

Birds are singing.

LUKE *goes to petrol pump. He takes matches from his pocket. Puts matches on the side of the pump.*

SETH *watches from behind a wrecked car. Something is going to happen ...*

LUKE *takes pump and turns on petrol.* LUKE *stares at the petrol for a while as it splashes to his feet. Then, almost ecstatically, he puts the end of the nozzle in his mouth.*

Petrol erupts from LUKE*'s mouth and nostrils. Then he starts covering himself in petrol.*

SETH *stares. He's transfixed. He wants to move, to say something, but he can't ...*

When LUKE*'s completely doused, he reaches for the matches. He takes one from the box and goes to strike it.*

It makes a scraping noise –

SETH *flinches!*

– but doesn't ignite.

LUKE *tries again!*

Scraping –

Flinch!

Doesn't ignite.

SETH *is trying so hard to speak.*

LUKE *goes to try again.*

Scrape –

SETH (*softly*): Pa!

LUKE: Son!

The match ignites!

EXT. GARAGE. NIGHT
Fire!

Red!

Sparks!

Noise!

33

The garage is an inferno!

Everything consumed with fire!

RUTH, SETH, JOSHUA *and the* DEPUTY *watch the blaze.*

LUKE *is obviously dead.*

SETH's *eyes are glinting with firelight. He's hypnotised by the horrific wonder of it . . .*

Sparks hover round him. It's a terrible sight, yes – but also one of the most beautiful he's ever seen. A fireworks display put on for his entertainment.

He becomes distracted by the sparks. They hover round him like glowing red insects, giant fire-flies. SETH *blows them . . .*

The sparks swirl in thermals of his breath.

EXT. WHEATFIELD. DAY

Yellow!

Dazzling yellow!

Cloudless sky.

Intensely blue.

And then –

SETH *runs through the field. He is wearing the American flag round his shoulders like a cloak. He runs and runs and runs until he reaches –*

EXT. PATH. DAY

– a path. He sees a figure in the distance. It is a young man – the young man from the photograph. It's CAMERON, SETH's *brother.*

CAMERON *is wearing a black suit, white shirt, his hair is jet black. There is a haunted quality about him. He has the good looks of a matinee idol, but a tired one. He is holding a suitcase.*

CAMERON *waves at* SETH. SETH *runs towards him. They meet and embrace.*

SETH: I missed you.

CAMERON: You look older.

SETH: You look old.

CAMERON: I do, eh?

SETH: Lots! ... You should have seen him, Cam. He
exploded. He went bang. His skin went all funny –

CAMERON: Don't think about it. Okay?

SETH: I dream it.

CAMERON *looks round at the endless wheatfields.*

CAMERON: God! It's ugly here! (*Snatches flag on* SETH's
shoulder.) What you wearing that for?

SETH: For you!

CAMERON: I don't want it.

SETH: Ain't you a hero?

CAMERON: No.

They walk away, hand in hand.

EXT. DOVE HOUSE. DAY
SETH *and* CAMERON *step onto porch.*

CAMERON: Jeez! This place get smaller?

SETH: No.

CAMERON: Still smells like gasoline.

SETH: I can't smell it.

CAMERON: That's because you smell like it too. (*Sees
harpoon.*) Where'd this come from?

SETH: Oh ... nowhere. Come on.

SETH *pulls* CAMERON *into house.*

SETH: You hungry, Cam?

CAMERON: No.

INT. DOVE HOUSE, KITCHEN. DAY
CAMERON *is sitting at table.* SETH *puts plate of cookies and
glass of milk in front of him.*

SETH: You miss 'em, Cam?

CAMERON: Miss what?

SETH: The Pretty Islands.

CAMERON: Could be.

SETH: You going back?

CAMERON: No. Suppose I'm staying.

SETH: That for good?

CAMERON: Might be I have to.

SETH: Why have to?

CAMERON: Look after you, knucklehead.

SETH: I don't need looking after.

CAMERON (*playfully*): Oh ... guess you want me to go –

> RUTH *enters. She is carrying a basket of washing, but we can see this is being done on automatic pilot. Her mind has gone.*

CAMERON: Hi, Ma.

> RUTH *looks at* CAMERON. *Something about him stirs her memory. Slowly, she embraces him.*
>
> CAMERON *is obviously uncomfortable with this intimacy. He bears it for as long as he can then struggles free, pushing* RUTH *aside.*

CAMERON (*angrily*): What, Ma? What do you want?

> *Instinctively,* RUTH *starts slapping at* CAMERON.

RUTH: Out of the way –

CAMERON: Stop it!

RUTH: Mind yourself!

CAMERON: Jesus!

RUTH: Gotta get the place clean. Your Pa'll be home soon.

CAMERON: Pa's dead! He's dead and buried, Ma!

EXT. GRAVEYARD. DAY

CAMERON *and* SETH *stand beside* LUKE's *grave.*

CAMERON: He was always reading. Nothing but those cheap pulps. Never said a word to me when I was a kid. Just sat there and got older. Couldn't stand the sight of blood. It was always Ma who killed the chickens. (*Kneels beside tombstone.*) You never stood a chance, Pa. You should have got out years ago. Before she drained you. (*At* SETH.) He wanted to be a beekeeper, you know that? It was her idea to start a garage –

Suddenly, a hideous, plastic hand rests on SETH'*s shoulder.* SETH *flinches, looks up and sees –*

SHERIFF TICKER *standing beside them. He's in his late fifties, with thin, greying hair. He's got one good eye (the bad one is covered with a silver patch), one hand and one ear.*

SHERIFF TICKER (*looking at grave*): Whiskers keep growing. When you're dead. Everything else stops but hair just keeps on sprouting. Hair never dies – just goes on and on ... (*At* CAMERON.) Heard you were back, Cameron.

CAMERON: Circumstances, Sheriff.

SHERIFF TICKER: Circumstances. Yes, sir. Ain't that the truth. I've been a Sheriff for over thirty years, and I've never seen so many circumstances. People stop me and say, 'Sheriff Ticker, what's happening?' And I have to say, 'I don't rightly know'. But it all starts with a kiss, that's for sure. Your Pa'll tell you.

CAMERON *stares, impassively.* SHERIFF TICKER *pats* SETH'*s head.*

SHERIFF TICKER: I wanna word with little Seth here. That okay with you?

CAMERON: Sure.

SHERIFF *leads* SETH *away towards –*

EXT. ROAD, NEAR GRAVEYARD. DAY

– where police car is parked. The DEPUTY *stands nearby.*
SHERIFF *leans against car and looks down at* SETH.

SHERIFF (*indicating false hand*): Turtle! Snapper it was. Big
as a pig and vicious as hell. Got my hand. Can you beat
that? Few years later, a dog almost chewed off my ear
... then a wasp stung out my eye. Thirty years a Sheriff
and all I've had to contend with are vicious animals. But
now ... (*Leans closer to* SETH.) ... we got a new kind of
animal. One I ain't seen before.
DOLPHIN *appears in distance, walking towards them.*
She's heading for graveyard, holding flowers.
SHERIFF: The kind of animal that does things to children.
Makes my hungry fish seem like an angel of mercy. The
only trouble is ... I ain't sure if the monster's still out
there somewhere. Or six feet under ... Perhaps your
father took secrets with him into that grave of his ...
DOLPHIN *passes them now. She looks back at* SETH.
SETH *stares at her.*
Then DOLPHIN *moves on. Towards the graveyard.*
Towards CAMERON –
SHERIFF: Your Pa ... Did he ever touch you?
SETH: Yeah.
SHERIFF: Where did he touch you, boy?
SETH: In the kitchen.
SHERIFF: No, no, no. I don't mean that ... Did he ever
touch you in places?
SETH: Places outside the kitchen?
SHERIFF: No, no, no. Places. On your person.
SETH: Like where?
SHERIFF: Like private places, boy.
SETH: Private places?

SHERIFF: Yeah ... Like here, boy.

> SHERIFF *touches between* SETH's *legs.* SETH *stares at* SHERIFF *for a beat.*

SETH: No. He didn't do much touching.

> SETH *looks at the graveyard.* DOLPHIN *is laying her flowers on a grave.* CAMERON *is moving towards her.*

SHERIFF: You go on back to your brother. You tell him to take care of you. You'll be safe with him.

> SETH *rushes to graveyard* –

EX. GRAVEYARD. DAY

– *where* DOLPHIN *and* CAMERON *are standing by Adam's* – DOLPHIN's *dead husband's* – *grave.*

DOLPHIN: I'm sorry about your father ... I saw the light of the burning from my window. I wondered what it was. It looked quite beautiful.

CAMERON: I bet it did.

DOLPHIN: Oh, that was a stupid thing to say. I'm sorry, Cameron.

CAMERON: Would you say that again?

DOLPHIN: What?

CAMERON: My name.

DOLPHIN: Cameron.

CAMERON: Sounds good. You know ... your accent. It makes everything sound better somehow.

DOLPHIN: Well, I ... I ...

CAMERON: Let me hear you say your name.

DOLPHIN: Dolphin Blue.

> CAMERON *looks at the remains of Adam's tombstone. It was obviously once an angel – but nothing much remains now. Just the feet and a broken wing.*

CAMERON: What happened? To the angel?

41

DOLPHIN: Oh ... Time! Even angels lose their wings eventually, I suppose.

SETH *rushes up and grabs* CAMERON's *hand.*

SETH (*urgently*): Cam!

DOLPHIN: Ah! There he is! My little demolition man.

CAMERON: Your what?

DOLPHIN: Seth knows what I mean.

SETH (*tugging at* CAMERON): Come on, Cam.

CAMERON: Get away from here. Go home and wait for me.

SETH: Cam!

CAMERON: Get out of here.

SETH: Don't talk to her.

CAMERON (*suddenly very angry*): Beat it!

DOLPHIN *smiles awkwardly and leaves.* CAMERON *watches her go.*

CAMERON (*at* SETH): I'm gonna kill you.

CAMERON *pushes* SETH *savagely to the ground, then follows* DOLPHIN *out of the graveyard.*

SETH *watches them go ...*

EXT. ABANDONED BARN. DAY

SETH *and* KIM *are walking towards the barn.*

KIM: My Ma says your Pa was a pervert.

SETH: What's a pervert?

KIM: Someone who likes children.

SETH: I don't think my Pa was a pervert then.

KIM: Nah. Nor mine.

SETH: My brother's back.

KIM: I know. Ma told me.

SETH: He met *her* today.

KIM: The vampire!

SETH: Yeah.

KIM: Did she bite his neck?

42

SETH: I don't know.

KIM: You think she wants to?

SETH: I guess so.

KIM: What you gonna do about it?

SETH: I don't know. Gotta do something.

KIM: You love your brother.

SETH: Yeah.

KIM: More than anything else in the world?

SETH: More than anything else in the world.

They go into the barn and –

INT. ABANDONED BARN. DAY
– start sniffing.

KIM: What's that smell?

SETH: I don't know.

They search. SETH *finds something buried beneath a pile of straw.*

SETH: Hey, Kim, look! I think I've found something.

It's a large ball of rolled up newspaper.

KIM: It looks like an egg.

They unwrap some of the paper. Inside they find a small, human figure. It's a foetus: eyes closed as if asleep. Skin wrinkled and mauve.

Flies buzz around it.

Maggots are on it.

KIM: It smells like fish.

SETH: You know what I think?

KIM: What?

SETH: I think we've found ourselves an angel.

KIM: An angel?

SETH *picks foetus up.*

SETH: Sure! And you know what?

KIM: What?

SETH: I think it could be Eben.

KIM: Eben! Why's Eben an angel?

SETH: 'Cos I told my Ma I missed Cameron. And made her cry. *That's* why Eben's an angel.

KIM: Who says?

SETH: It's just so, Kim.

KIM: Well . . . it sure looks like Eben. But if Eben's an angel, why ain't he in heaven?

SETH: 'Cos he was murdered! Murdered angels don't go to heaven. They get their wings torn out and are thrown back to earth again.

KIM: Who says?

SETH: It's just so, Kim. (*Looks at back of foetus.*) There! You see? That's where its wings were.

KIM: Poor Eben.

SETH *goes to leave the barn.*

KIM (*angrily*): Where you going?

SETH: Home.

KIM: You can't have the angel.

SETH (*angrily*): Why not?

KIM: He belongs to me. He was my friend.

SETH: He was my friend too.

KIM: He liked me more!

SETH: You made him cry!

KIM: So did you! I wanna keep it!

SETH: I found it!

KIM: I saw it first!

SETH: I unwrapped it!

KIM: I started it!

SETH: I walked this way!

KIM: I –

SETH *viciously pushes* KIM *to the ground.*

SETH: I keep the angel.

SETH *marches out of the barn, clutching foetus.*

INT. DOVE HOUSE, SETH'S BEDROOM. DAY

SETH *is sitting on bed. The foetus is laying beside him.*

SETH (*at foetus*): What are we gonna do, Eben? She's met
    him now: my brother. She's gonna suck his blood and
    kill him just like she killed you ... (*Leans closer to foetus,
    as if it's speaking to him.*) ... What? She did that? ... Bit
    your neck. I know, Eben, I know. That's what vampires
    are like. I know ... But I'm watching her. Don't worry.
    I'm watching. Everything. Everything.

CAMERON (*off*): Seth? You here?

SETH (*at foetus*): You be quiet now.

    SETH *puts foetus in small wooden box.*

SETH: I'll be back, Eben.

    He hides the box under his bed, then goes to –

INT. DOVE HOUSE, KITCHEN. DAY

– where CAMERON *is washing his face at sink.* SETH *sits at
table.*

CAMERON: What the Sheriff want?

SETH: Nothing.

CAMERON: Long while about nothing.

    SETH *is sulking.*

CAMERON: You okay?

SETH: I suppose.

CAMERON: Look ... I'm sorry I pushed you, okay? It's just
    that sometimes ... well, you're not wanted.

    SETH *doesn't respond.* CAMERON *sits at table with him.*

CAMERON: Want see something?

    CAMERON *takes wallet from his pocket and removes a
    photograph. It is of a soldier holding a badly burnt baby.*

CAMERON: What you make of that?

SETH: What is it?

46

CAMERON: It's a baby.

SETH: What happened to him?

CAMERON: Well ... he lived in a place in Japan. It's skin got all silver and shiny. Just like a mirror. You could see your face in it.

SETH: Why?

CAMERON: Just could.

SETH: Did it hurt?

CAMERON: Yeah ... I guess.

SETH: Is he alive?

CAMERON: Yeah.

SETH: You know him?

CAMERON: No. It's just a photograph.

> CAMERON *is looking uncomfortable now. He wasn't expecting questions like this.*

SETH: Who's holding him?

CAMERON: I don't know.

SETH: Did he have any brothers like you're my brother?

> CAMERON's *discomfort is turning to irritation.*

CAMERON: I don't know, Seth. It's just a picture.

SETH: What's his name?

CAMERON: I don't know his name. It's just a photograph, okay?

SETH: But he must have had a name.

> *Now* CAMERON's *irritation becomes anger ...*

CAMERON: He must have had a shoe size too, but I don't know that either. It's just a picture of a baby.

> SETH *rummages in* CAMERON's *wallet. He finds two other photos. One is a photo of a naked blonde girl in a very provocative pose. The other is of* CAMERON *and* SETH.

CAMERON: You like 'em? You can have them ... And, before you ask – (*Indicates photo of blonde girl.*) – I don't know her name either.

> CAMERON *leaves.*

47

SETH *stares at the three photographs. Something is going on in his head. As if the photographs pose a riddle he has to solve.*

Bomb victim.

Naked girl.

Family ...

Somewhere, in these three images, is an answer ...

If only he knew the question.

EXT. DOVE HOUSE. NIGHT

Moonlight bathes the house.

Insects chirp and buzz.

One window is illuminated. SETH*'s bedroom where –*

INT. DOVE HOUSE, SETH'S BEDROOM. NIGHT

– SETH *is sitting up in bed. His face full of worry and fear. He clutches the catapult-crucifix for comfort.*

There's a noise outside ... A howling dog, an owl, something that intensifies SETH*'s growing unease. He clutches the crucifix tighter.*

The bedside lamp flickers once, twice, then goes out altogether.

SETH *whimpers in the barely moonlit room. Holding the crucifix to his chest, he disappears beneath the sheets of his bed.*

He lays there, crying with fear ...

SETH: Go away!

Go away!

Go away!

EXT. SUNRISE. DAY

The sun is rising.

A monstrous ball of fire on the horizon.

48

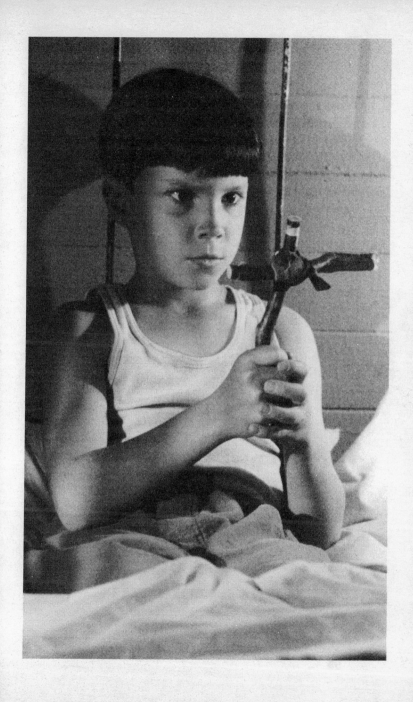

The sky is bright orange.
An inferno ...

INT. DOVE HOUSE, SETH'S BEDROOM. DAY
SETH *is asleep. He still clutches the crucifix.*

CAMERON (*from downstairs*): Seth!
    SETH's *eyes click open.*
CAMERON (*from downstairs*): I'm just going out for a while.
    Downstairs: the front door opens and closes. SETH *dashes*
    to the window, opens it, looks out, sees –

EX. DOVE HOUSE. DAY
– CAMERON *is walking away from the house.* SETH *is at*
bedroom window, watching him.

SETH: Where you going?
CAMERON (*irritably*): I'm going up to Dolphin's house.
    Jesus!
    CAMERON *leaves frame.*
      SETH *stares after him for a beat, then –*

INT. DOVE HOUSE, SETH'S BEDROOM. DAY
– he quickly closes window. SETH *hurriedly starts dressing.*

EXT. DOLPHIN'S HOUSE. DAY
Yellow wheat.
    Blue sky.
    White house.
    Towards which SETH *runs. He is flustered, panicking a*
little. He rushes up to the house. Tries the window where he got
in before. It's locked.
    He looks round, frustrated. Goes to front of house. Front door

is locked too!

He looks up at the house. What's going on? His brother is in there! With DOLPHIN. *The Vampire. He needs to get to him as soon as possible. Watch him. Protect him.*

SETH *goes round to the side door. It opens.*

SETH *goes inside and –*

INT. DOLPHIN'S HOUSE, BACK ROOM. DAY

– looks around. Again, the contents are incongruous with the outside: sea shells, shark jaws, piranhas.

SETH *goes into –*

INT. DOLPHIN'S HOUSE, MAIN ROOM. DAY

– and sees ...

Sea shells.

Shark jaws.

Piranhas.

The photograph of Adam.

But ... where are CAMERON *and* DOLPHIN? SETH *is lost, bewildered. Where?* Where? *And then –*

Voices from upstairs. SETH *goes –*

INT. DOLPHIN'S HOUSE, STAIRS. DAY

– and listens at DOLPHIN's *bedroom. Yes:* DOLPHIN *and* CAMERON *are inside.*

SETH *sits on top step, waiting. Listening to –*

INT. DOLPHIN'S HOUSE, DOLPHIN'S BEDROOM. DAY

CAMERON *and* DOLPHIN *are on either side of the bed.* DOLPHIN *has been showing* CAMERON *some old photographs.*

DOLPHIN: Oh, it was really quite beautiful, you know.
The war in London. All that noise and fire, people
huddled together. Laughter and cuddles.

CAMERON: You like those bombs, don't you?

DOLPHIN: Oh, I love them. All that noise ... explosions.

CAMERON: I've seen the big ones, you know. Lots of them.
The biggest ones there are.

DOLPHIN: Where?

CAMERON: In the Pacific. That's where I've been. The
Pretty Islands, as my Ma calls them.

DOLPHIN: What have you been doing there?

CAMERON: Blowing them up.

DOLPHIN: Whole islands?

CAMERON: Well, yeah ... whole islands.

DOLPHIN: I ... I bet it was ... well, dangerous.

CAMERON: Not really. We watched from a distance. God!
It was bright. I mean, bright like you've never seen.
Like a million Fourths of July, all rolled into one. The
natives paddled out in their canoes, and they were
singing, 'You are my sunshine, my only sunshine ... '
And there'd be this stuff like silver snow falling on the
ship. We'd roll it up and have snowball fights with it.
And after each blast the sea would be full of boiled fish.
You could pick them up and eat them if you wanted to.
And the sunsets ... the sunsets were ... pink. Bright
pink. Pink like you've never seen.

*There's a long silence after this. It's been like a confession
for* CAMERON, *a prayer. It's touched both him, and*
DOLPHIN.

   DOLPHIN *stares at him, sensing his inner-grief, his loss.
She recognises it as her own.*

   DOLPHIN *goes to* CAMERON. CAMERON *has his
head bowed.* DOLPHIN *raises his head gently ...*

DOLPHIN: Cameron ... Cameron, look at me.

Slowly – oh, so slowly – DOLPHIN *kisses* CAMERON. *It*

is painfully tender. A kiss on the verge of heartbreak.

At first CAMERON *doesn't respond. But then – again, slowly – he does. He must kiss her or be lonely forever.*

DOLPHIN *unbuttons* CAMERON'*s shirt. His skin is flawless, smooth. It's a wonder to her. She runs her fingers over its thrilling perfection . . .*

Meanwhile, outside –

INT. DOLPHIN'S HOUSE, STAIRS. DAY
– SETH *has become aware that the voices have stopped. Curiously – and a little worried – he pushes open the door just a little. And he sees –*

INT. DOLPHIN'S HOUSE, DOLPHIN'S BEDROOM. DAY
CAMERON, *half-naked, is in* DOLPHIN'*s arms. To* SETH'*s eyes, it looks as if she possesses him totally.*

INT. DOLPHIN'S HOUSE, STAIRS. DAY
SETH *panics. What to do? To stay and help, or –*

Run!

That's what he does . . .

Run! Run! Run!

He runs away from the vampire's victory. Runs down the stairs –

INT. DOLPHIN'S HOUSE, MAIN ROOM. DAY
– and runs through the room. To the front door. Unlocks it. Runs out –

53

EXT. DOLPHIN'S HOUSE. DAY

– and runs away from the house. SETH *cuts a path through the yellow wheat. He is whimpering with panic and fear. He runs, runs, runs –*

EXT. ROAD THROUGH WHEATFIELD. DAY

– until he is breathless and gleaming with sweat.

In the distance, he sees KIM. KIM *has just found the American flag* CAMERON *had discarded earlier. He's putting it round his shoulders.*

SETH (*calling*): Kim! Kim!

> KIM *sees* SETH *and begins walking towards him. And then –*
>> *The black Cadillac appears. It's heading down an adjacent road. Straight for* KIM ...

SETH: Kim!

> *The Cadillac pulls up beside* KIM. *The* DRIVER *and the other three* YOUNG MEN *get out.*

DRIVER (*at* KIM): Hey, you ... Come here!

> SETH *can only hear this faintly. It's too far away to do anything. He's also frozen with horror now, because the* DRIVER *grabs* KIM, *punches the child violently.*
>
> *The* YOUNG MEN *are whooping and cheering.* KIM *is kicking and screaming. But the* YOUNG MEN *are stronger. They throw him in the back of the car.* KIM's *muffled cries can be heard.*
>
> *The* YOUNG MEN *are almost hysterical with excitement. They get in the car. It drives away ... Dust spews up behind.* KIM's *screams grow fainter.*
>
> SETH *watches the car disappear.*
>
> *Dust.*
>
> *Screams ...*
>
> *The car disappears. Dust settles. Screams fade away.*

Just silence ...
Silence and ...
Yellow wheat ...
Blue sky.
And SETH's *horrified eyes!*
And in the horrified eyes ...
Yellow wheat!
Blue sky.
Yellow wheat.
Blue sky. And ...
Horror ...
Slow fade to black.

EXT. WHEATFIELD. SUNRISE
The sun is blood red.
   Sky orange.
   Clouds, yellow.
   The wheat shimmers gold ...

INT. DOVE HOUSE, SETH'S BEDROOM. DAY
SETH *asleep in bed, entangled in a sweaty mass of sheets. He's obviously had a restless night. He's still tossing and turning a little. The sheets get more and more tangled until, at last, he wakes up. He blinks against the early morning light, untangles himself, then sits on the edge of the mattress for a while. Rubbing his eyes, he leaves the room, and –*

INT. DOVE'S HOUSE, BATHROOM. DAY
– walks into the bathroom, still bleary-eyed.
   He slooshes his faces with water, then – he notices
CAMERON's *comb. He picks it up. Looks at it. Pulls strands of hair from between the prongs.*

56

SETH (*horrified*): His hair! It is his hair!
   Panicking, he rushes out and back into –

INT. DOVE HOUSE, SETH'S BEDROOM. DAY
– and gets the foetus from under the bed. Starts talking to it with the familiarity of a best friend.

SETH: Look! It's happening! She's killing him! Look! Cameron will end up in a black box. Just like her dead husband. Bits of hair. Teeth. His sweat in a bottle ... What am I going to do, Eben? What? I've got to tell him, Eben. Otherwise ... she'll kill him –
   SETH *is interruped by –*

EXT. DOVE HOUSE. DAY

JOSHUA: Murderer!
   JOSHUA's *obviously taken to drink since the death of his son,* EBEN. *He's unshaven, hair dishevelled and his clothes are filthy.*
   JOSHUA *picks up rock and throws it –*

INT. DOVE HOUSE, SETH'S BEDROOM. DAY
– at the house.
   Crash!
   SETH *is startled. For a split second, he freezes, then he rushes out of the room and into –*

INT. DOVE HOUSE, CAMERON'S BEDROOM. DAY
– where CAMERON *is fast asleep. He is peaceful, huddled in a tight, foetal position, sheets wrapped round him like a cocoon.*
   SETH *jumps on the bed and starts shaking him.*

57

SETH: Wake up, Cam! Wake up!

CAMERON: What ... ? What ... ?

JOSHUA (*off*): Come out!

> *Another rock smashes through the window. CRASH!*
>> CAMERON *jumps out of bed, shocked.*

CAMERON: What the ... ?

EXT. DOVE HOUSE. DAY

JOSHUA *is preparing to throw another brick.* CAMERON, *followed by* SETH, *runs out.*

JOSHUA: Murderer! Murderer! –

CAMERON: What you playing at, Josh? What's the matter with you? God dammit –

> CAMERON *slaps the brick from* JOSHUA's *hand.*

JOSHUA: I wanna see him!

CAMERON: See who?

JOSHUA: The killer!

CAMERON: There's no killer here.

JOSHUA: Bring him! He's a coward!

CAMERON (*at* SETH): What's he talking about?

SETH: Pa, I guess.

CAMERON (*at* JOSH): Pa's dead, Josh.

JOSHUA: He's not dead.

CAMERON: What are you talking about?

> RUTH *now appears on the porch. She is trembling with fear.* JOSHUA *points at her angrily.*

JOSHUA: *She's* hiding him.

> CAMERON *grabs* JOSHUA *by the lapels and shakes him.*

CAMERON: Bullshit! You can't hide a corpse, Josh! Now, come on, you've been drinking. Just go home.

JOSHUA: Ain't no home, Cameron. People all gone. God took them 'cos of my wicked thoughts.

CAMERON: You ain't got wicked thoughts, Josh. Just ... bad luck.

JOSHUA: Oh, you don't know! My thoughts ... Jesus! They're bad. I dreamt ... I dreamt that I was sleeping with my goat. And I *liked* it!

CAMERON: Well, you could do worse. (*At* SETH.) Get Ma inside.

SETH *goes to* RUTH.

JOSHUA: Where is he, Ruth? Bring him to me!

SETH: Punch him, Cam!

CAMERON: Shut up!

SETH: You can do it!

CAMERON: He's just drunk!

JOSHUA: What's it like, boy?

CAMERON: What's what like?

JOSHUA: To know your Pa's a killer.

CAMERON (*getting angry now*): Pa is no killer! Come on! He's dead! Snap out of it.

JOSHUA: He took my Eben.

CAMERON: No. He didn't.

SETH: They all say that, Cam.

CAMERON *is surprised by* SETH's *almost flippant tone.*

CAMERON: And you believe them?

SETH: I don't know. Was Pa a pervert?

CAMERON: A what? What do you mean – ?

JOSHUA, *making the most of* CAMERON's *distraction, pushes by and rushes at* RUTH –

JOSHUA: RUUUUTHHH!

RUTH *screams.* JOSHUA *grabs her round the throat and starts throttling her.*

JOSHUA: Where is he? I wanna hurt him. I want to suck out his eyes –

CAMERON *dashes to* JOSHUA. *Grabs him. Pulls him from* RUTH.

JOSHUA *punches* CAMERON. *It's a hard vicious punch*

and it takes CAMERON *by surprise.* CAMERON *falls to the floor.*

SETH *rushes at* JOSHUA *and starts hitting him.* JOSHUA *kicks* SETH *aside, then grabs the harpoon on the porch.*

CAMERON *goes for* JOSHUA *again.* JOSHUA *fights with harpoon, swinging it in wide, vicious arcs.* SETH *is laying on the ground, dazed.*

RUTH *is screaming.*

CAMERON *and* JOSHUA *continue to struggle. It's a rough, chaotic scrabble. At one point, instinctively,* CAMERON *grabs the end of the harpoon. As* JOSHUA *pulls it free,* CAMERON's *hand is cut across palm.* CAMERON *yells in pain and punches* JOSHUA *hard on the jaw.* JOSHUA *collapses, unconscious.*

INT. DOVE HOUSE, KITCHEN. DAY

SETH *and* CAMERON *are at table.* SETH *is bathing* CAMERON's *cut hand. It's nothing serious, just a deep graze.* RUTH *sits on sofa, trembling, in a world of her own.*

Sound of footsteps on porch!

Everyone looks up, nervous – Knock on door!

RUTH *lets out a whimper.* SETH *glances at* CAMERON, *worried.*

CAMERON (*at* RUTH): Get the door, Ma.

RUTH *doesn't move.*

CAMERON: What you afraid of? Go on! See who it is!

RUTH, *timorously, opens door.*

DOLPHIN *is standing there. She's dressed in a soft, grey dress now. And she looks younger, brighter, more relaxed. The hidden beauty we suspected earlier has now declared itself.*

DOLPHIN: Can I see him?

RUTH glances at CAMERON, then opens the door wider.

DOLPHIN dashes in.

DOLPHIN: Cameron!

CAMERON: Oh, hi! Come in!

DOLPHIN rushes to CAMERON and kneels beside him, pushing her way in between the two brothers.

DOLPHIN: You alright?

CAMERON: Oh, yeah. It's nothing.

DOLPHIN takes CAMERON's wounded hand from SETH.

DOLPHIN: Oh, God.

CAMERON: It's nothing.

DOLPHIN indicating the bowl of water, antiseptic and plasters etc.

DOLPHIN (*to SETH*): Shall I do that?

SETH (*firmly*): No!

SETH continues bathing CAMERON's hand, trying his best to push DOLPHIN out of the way. CAMERON and DOLPHIN are lost in each other.

DOLPHIN: They said it was … I mean, I thought –

CAMERON: Oh, it was just Josh. Nothing. I told you. Nothing.

DOLPHIN and CAMERON stare at each other lovingly.

CAMERON: You look beautiful.

Unable to restrain themselves, they kiss. SETH glares at them. They continue kissing, oblivious.

SETH digs a cotton bud savagely into CAMERON's wound. CAMERON stops kissing and –

CAMERON: That hurt!

CAMERON pushes SETH away. SETH goes to the end of the table as DOLPHIN and CAMERON embrace –

CAMERON: I really missed you.

They kiss even more passionately.

SETH glares at them. This time the look is neither panic,

*nor fear. It's hatred. Undiluted hatred. For this woman
who has such power over his brother ...*

EXT. ABANDONED HOUSES. DAY
*A few ramshackle houses in the middle of nowhere. There's a
police car.* SHERIFF TICKER *is leaning against the bonnet. He
is trying to calm a tearful, near hysterical, woman. This is*
CASSIE, KIM's *mother.*

The DEPUTY *is searching the abandoned houses.* SETH
appears and CASSIE *immediately pounces at him –*

CASSIE: Him! Him!

SHERIFF: Now, Cassie!

CASSIE: Ask him!

SHERIFF (*at* SETH): Seth! Have you seen Kim?

SETH: No.

CASSIE: He's lying.

SHERIFF: You lying?

CASSIE: Of course he is. I can tell. You ain't got no kids.
    You don't know their ways.

SHERIFF (*at* SETH): Tell me the truth, son.

SETH: I am.

CASSIE: I tell you! He's hiding my Kim.

SHERIFF: You hiding him, boy?

SETH: No!

    CASSIE *rushes to* SETH *and grabs him.*

CASSIE: You know what you're full of, Seth Dove?

SETH: No, ma'am.

CASSIE: Sin! Ain't that right?

SETH: I don't know, ma'am.

CASSIE: Well, I'm telling you, boy. You're full of sin! Say it!
    Sin! Say it! Sin! Sin!

SETH: Sin!

CASSIE: Louder!

62

SETH: Sin!

CASSIE: Again!

SETH: Sin!

CASSIE: Again! Again!

SETH: Sin! Sin!

SHERIFF pulls CASSIE from SETH.

CASSIE (*at* SHERIFF): Look at him! He's enjoying it! Can't you see he's enjoying it! He's a monster –

The DEPUTY appears from inside one of the abandoned buildings. He's holding the body of KIM, wrapped in the American flag. CASSIE screams and runs to him. She takes the body of her dead child and collapses to her knees.

CASSIE: What's killing all the children? What's killing the children?

The SHERIFF grabs SETH by the shoulders and looks at him intensely.

SHERIFF: Every cop in the state's on the job, and you know what I think?

SETH: No.

SHERIFF: I think your Pa's still out there. Dripping gasoline and killing children. And you wanna know what else I think?

SETH: What?

SHERIFF: I think you've got secrets locked up in here – (*Taps SETH's head with his plastic hand.*) – and it's my job to get them out. Even if I have to crack you open like a peanut. You understand me?

SETH: Yeah.

SHERIFF: Well, I hope you do. 'Cos whatever you got up here – (*Another tap.*) – I'm gonna find out. One way or another. I'm gonna get it out.

SHERIFF TICKER helps DEPUTY get CASSIE, still clutching the dead KIM, into the car. It drives away.

SETH watches it disappear into the distance . . . Dust spews up behind the car.

63

Dust.
   Yellow.
   Blue.
   Silence.

INT. DOVE HOUSE. DAY

SETH *is sitting at table.* CAMERON *enters* ...

CAMERON: Look in my mouth.

SETH: What?

CAMERON: My mouth.

SETH: What is it?

CAMERON: Can you see anything? I can taste blood.

SETH: It's your gums.

CAMERON: My gums?

SETH: Yeah. They're bleeding.

CAMERON: I'm losing weight as well. You know I had to
   take my belt in two notches.

SETH: You going bald too?

CAMERON: I'm going bald.

SETH: I found hair in your comb.

CAMERON: Does it show? I mean, can you tell by looking at
   me.

SETH: No. Not really.

CAMERON: How old do I look?

SETH: You look twenty-six.

CAMERON: Don't be stupid! You're just saying that 'cos you
   know. Nobody looks twenty-six, for chrissakes.

   CAMERON *sits on sofa.* SETH *watches him for a moment.*
   Then –

SETH: Cam! I gotta tell you something.

CAMERON: What now?

   SETH *joins* CAMERON *on sofa.*

SETH: Cam –

CAMERON: What?

SETH: Cam, I know why you're getting old.

CAMERON: Why?

SETH: 'Cos of her.

CAMERON: Who?

SETH: Dolphin.

CAMERON: What you mean?

SETH: She's a vampire.

CAMERON: She's a vampire.

SETH: I knew you wouldn't believe me.

CAMERON: Oh, sure –

SETH: She's a vampire! And she's drinking your blood.

CAMERON: Mmm.

SETH: You don't see that, do you?

CAMERON: Oh, yeah.

SETH: Listen! That is why you're getting older and she's getting younger.

CAMERON: You're crazy.

SETH: It's true!

CAMERON: You really believe that?

SETH: Yeah.

CAMERON: You're out of your mind.

SETH: It's true, Cam.

    CAMERON *stands up.*

CAMERON: I can't listen to this crap anymore.

SETH: Cam!

CAMERON: Leave me alone.

SETH: Cam! Come back!

    CAMERON *leaves.* SETH *gets up and –*

EXT. DOVE HOUSE. DAY

– rushes after CAMERON. CAMERON *walks away from house, angrily.* SETH *chases after him.*

65

SETH: Cam! Stop! Don't leave me! You can't go.

CAMERON: Just watch me!

SETH: You can't leave me with Ma.

CAMERON: Oh, shut up! She's better than before. Does the cooking and the housework and keeps her mouth shut. What more do you want?

SETH: You can't go with Dolphin. She's a vampire. She'll kill you. I'm warning you –

CAMERON (*grabbing* SETH): Shut up! Listen, you little bastard, I love her. You understand? I love her. And she loves me. And I'm going away with her and be happy. And there's not a damn thing you can do about it. You understand me? You hear me?

SETH *nods*.

CAMERON: Now shut up!

CAMERON *walks away. Lost,* SETH *watches him go.*
Yellow.
Blue.
Silence.
And a disappearing brother ...

EXT. DOVE HOUSE. NIGHT
Moonlight bathes the house.

INT. DOVE HOUSE, SETH'S BEDROOM. NIGHT
SETH *is lying in bed, talking to the foetus.*

SETH: She's got him now, Eben. And there's nothing I can do. She's won and I've lost. She's gonna kill him, Eben. (*Leans closer to foetus, as if it's talking to him again.*) What? Say that again ...
Tell me ...
Tell me ...
Tell me ...

66

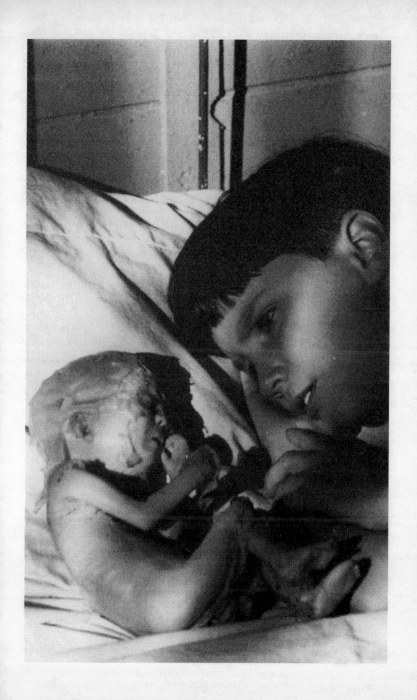

EXT. MOON. NIGHT

The moon is a blue orb.

SETH (*voice over*): Tell me ...
    Tell me ...
    Tell me ...

Slow dissolve to ...

EXT. SUN. DAY

... The moon dissolves into the sun. Night becomes day ...
    Black to blue.
    Dark to yellow.
    Yellow.

EXT. CROSSROADS. DAY

It is a brilliant summer's day.
    Yellow wheatfields. Yellow for as far as the eye can see. Too yellow.
    A flat, blue sky. Endless blue. Too blue.
    In the distance, farmhouses gleam white and silver. Too white. Too silver.
    Someone is walking towards us. The figure is indistinct, shimmering like a ghost in summer heat. It is DOLPHIN. *She is wearing white now, her hair is golden as the wheat, and she looks radiant, young and very, very happy.* DOLPHIN *stands at the crossroads, waiting for something. She wipes perspiration from her brow with a delicate lace handkerchief.*
    Insects buzz ...
    Birds chirp ...
    The heat pulsates ...
    A langorous heat.
    Yellow.
    Blue.

Silver.

White.

SETH *appears. He hesitates slightly when he sees* DOLPHIN, *then approaches her. She is lost in her thoughts, the heat, and doesn't see him —*

SETH: Dolphin.

DOLPHIN *looks at* SETH. *She smiles, pleased.*

SETH: You waiting for something?

DOLPHIN: Yes. For a ride. I'm going to town.

SETH *looks up at her.* DOLPHIN *kneels in front of him.*

DOLPHIN: I love him, you know. Really. I'll look after him. He'll be safe with me.

SETH *stares, not saying a word.*

Insects buzz ...

Birds chirp ...

The heat ...

Yellow ...

Blue ...

Yellow ...

Blue ...

DOLPHIN (*softly*): Poor Seth! It's all so horrible, isn't it? The nightmare of childhood. And it only gets worse. One day you'll wake up and you'll be past it. Your beautiful skin will wrinkle and shrivel up. You'll lose your hair. Your sight. Your memory. Your blood will thicken. Teeth turn yellow and loose. You'll start to stink and fart and all your friends will be dead. You'll succumb to arthritis. Angina. Senile dementia. You'll piss yourself. Shit yourself. Drool at the mouth. Just pray that when this happens, you've got someone to love you. Because, if you're loved, you'll still be young ... Oh, innocence can be hell.

As DOLPHIN *speaks,* SETH *looks over her shoulder and sees — The black Cadillac approaching. It glints black and cold in the heat. Gets closer ... Closer ...*

  Insects ...
  Birds ...
  Heat ...
  Yellow ...
  Blue ...
  The black Cadillac.

  DOLPHIN *is stroking* SETH's *cheek. Touches his hair. His mouth. She is smiling at him, her speech like a lullaby to soothe a distressed child.*

  On the word 'hell' the Cadillac pulls up beside. The DRIVER *winds down the window. He, and the other three* YOUNG MEN, *smile at* SETH *like old friends.*

DRIVER: Well, well, well, if it isn't the scarecrow's son. You wanna ride, Seth Dove?

SETH: Not yet.

DOLPHIN: Where are you boys going?

DRIVER: Where *you* going?

DOLPHIN: To town.

DRIVER (*to young men*): We going that way, boys?

  A general chorus of assent.

DRIVER (*at* DOLPHIN): Looks like we're going that way.

DOLPHIN: Thanks.

  One of the YOUNG MEN *opens the door for* DOLPHIN. *She goes to get in. As she does so ... She smiles at* SETH.
    SETH *stays back.*
    Insects.
    Birds.
    Heat ...
    The car door slams behind DOLPHIN.

DRIVER (*at* SETH): It's a beautiful day, isn't it, Seth Dove?

SETH (*smiling*): Yeah.

  The car drives away, billowing smoke behind it. SETH *watches it go. His eyes are calm.*

70

Yellow.
Blue.
Insects . . .

Slow fade to black.

EXT. DOVE HOUSE. DAY
SETH, CAMERON *and* RUTH *are sitting on porch. They are each lost in their own thoughts.* SETH *is staring at the harpoon.* CAMERON *is gazing at the blue sky.* RUTH *is searching for her lost sanity.*

The sun beats down. No breeze. Everything very still. Insects.

SETH *looks at* CAMERON, *worried.* CAMERON *becomes aware of this look.*

CAMERON: What you looking at?
SETH: Nothing.
CAMERON: Don't look like nothing.
A long beat.
Insects . . .
Heat . . .
Very still . . .
CAMERON: Why don't you go play with your friends?
SETH: They're all dead.
Another long beat.
Insects . . .
Heat . . .
Very still . . .
And then – CAMERON *sees something – It looks like the* SHERIFF's *car and a few people are in the nearby field.*
CAMERON (*standing*): What's the Sheriff's car doing down there?
CAMERON *stands, leaves the porch.* SETH *chases after him.*
72

SETH: Cam! Wait, Cam!

RUTH *follows them ...*

SETH: Cam! Wait! Wait!

EXT. NEARBY FIELD. DAY

SETH *chases after* CAMERON. *He knows what* CAMERON *will find in the field. He tugs at* CAMERON's *clothes.*

SETH: Come home, Cam.

CAMERON: Leave me alone.

SETH: Don't go there!

CAMERON: What do you mean? Leave me alone!

CAMERON *and* SETH *get closer to the police car.*

Now we see ... DOLPHIN *is lying on the ground. She is dead. Her white dress is spotless. She looks very peaceful, like a sleeping swan.*

The SHERIFF *stands nearby. As does* JOSHUA *and* CAMERON *and a few bystanders.* CAMERON *cries out in shock.*

SETH: Cam!

CAMERON *runs to body. The* SHERIFF *tries to stop him –*

SHERIFF: Don't, son! Leave her!

– but CAMERON *pushes him aside.* CAMERON *grabs* DOLPHIN's *dead body. He weeps hysterically.* RUTH *tries to pull* CAMERON *away –*

CAMERON (*screaming*): No!

– but, again, he pushes her aside.

SETH *stares in rising horror. Yes,* DOLPHIN *is dead. This is what he wanted. But he hadn't expected this reaction from* CAMERON. *Not this grief ... Not this –*

CAMERON: Noooooooo!

SETH *runs away from the nightmare ...*

EXT. BARREN FIELD. SUNSET

The sky is blood red.

SETH *runs into shot, falls to his knees. He is hysterical. His face full of terror. A terror he's never known before. A terror he could never have imagined ... He stares at the setting sun.*

Red! Red! Red!

He screams. It's a scream from the centre of him. A primaeval howl of despair – The scream echoes endlessly.

The sun sets further.

SETH *screams at the setting sun. Screams for all his worth. Screams against the impending dark ...*

Sunset!
Scream!
Sunset!
Scream!
Scream!
Scream!

Cut to black.
Hold black.
Silence.
Roll credits.

THE PASSION OF DARKLY NOON

'The human heart is a dark forest.'

Tobias Wolff

CAST

DARKLY NOON	Brendan Fraser
CALLIE	Ashley Judd
CLAY	Viggo Mortensen
JUDE	Loren Dean
ROXY	Grace Zabriskie
QUINCY	Lou Meyers
MA	Kate Harper
PA	Mel Cobb
RINGMASTER	Josse de Pauw

Written & Directed by	Philip Ridley
Producers	Dominic Anciano
	Frank Henschke
Co-Executive Producer	Shelly Bancroft
Director of Photography	John de Borman
Music	Nick Bicât
Editor	Leslie Healey
Production Design	Hubert Pouille
Sound Design	Nigel Galt
Costume Designer	Gabi Binder

'Who Will Love Me Now?'
Written by Nick Bicât & Philip Ridley
Performed by P.J. Harvey
(*Courtesy of Island Records*)

'Look What You've Done (To My Skin)'
Written by Nick Bicât & Philip Ridley
Performed by Gavin Friday
(*Courtesy of Island Records*)

First Day

EXT. MOUNTAINS. DAWN
A ridge of mountains: primordial, timeless.

EXT. ROCKY PLATEAUX. AFTERNOON
A young man, in his early twenties, clambers over the rocks. He is dressed in a silvery-grey suit, white shirt and tie. Everything is dirty and worn through. A tear at his knee reveals a cut leg. The young man has pale, delicate features. An almost painful innocence contrasts starkly with his shock of black, dishevelled hair. He is walking awkwardly, as if delirious with fever. Sweat trickles down his unshaven face. His name is DARKLY NOON.

DARKLY *staggers up over the rocks. Then onwards...*

EXT. ROAD THROUGH FOREST. AFTERNOON
A Chevrolet truck is thundering down the road. By the look of the truck we can see we're in the present day ...

EXT. FOREST. AFTERNOON
DARKLY *is stumbling in the forest. He obviously doesn't know where he's going. He's walking for the sake of walking, walking as if his life depended on it. The trees get denser and denser.* DARKLY *slips and starts half-sliding, half-walking down a steep hill ...*

EXT. ROAD THROUGH FOREST. AFTERNOON
A Chevrolet truck is still thundering down the path. It's being driven by ...

EXT./INT. INSIDE TRUCK, ROAD THROUGH FOREST.
AFTERNOON
A young man named JUDE. *He is good-looking with wide, open
country boy looks, as wholesome as apple pie. He's alone in the
truck, only half looking where he's going. It's a route he's taken
many times before ...*

EXT. FOREST. AFTERNOON
DARKLY *stumbles ...*

EXT. ROAD THROUGH FOREST. AFTERNOON
Truck thunders ...

EXT. FOREST. AFTERNOON
Stumbles ...

EXT. ROAD THROUGH FOREST. AFTERNOON
Thunders ...

EXT. FOREST. AFTERNOON
DARKLY's *feet get entangled in the undergrowth ... He
tumbles ...*

EXT. ROAD THROUGH FOREST. AFTERNOON
Thunders ...

EXT. FOREST. AFTERNOON
Tumbles ...

80

EXT. ROAD THROUGH FOREST. AFTERNOON
The truck thunders round a corner. It nearly runs over
DARKLY *laying in its path.* JUDE *swerves violently. The truck*
screeches to a sudden halt.

JUDE (*getting out of the truck*): What the ... ?
    He rushes to DARKLY ... *Feels* DARKLY'*s forehead.*
JUDE: Hey, you alright?
    DARKLY'*s eyes flutter open ...*
DARKLY: Oh God! Help me ...
    JUDE *carefully picks* DARKLY *up. He carries him over to*
    the truck. He can't put him in the passenger seat because
    it's full of supplies, so he puts him in the back.
    DARKLY'*s eyes feverishly open. He sees –*

EXT. BRANCHES AGAINST THE SKY. AFTERNOON
– the forest is closing in above, less and less sky can be seen.

TITLE: WHITE ON BLACK
    THE PASSION OF DARKLY NOON

EXT. CALLIE'S HOMESTEAD. DAY
A clearing in the forest.
    We see a neat, two storey house, built for a family. It's
predominantly white, with silver roof. There's a porch with
swing chair, table, chairs. Everything very welcoming. A barn
is nearby: again, white and silver.
    The truck pulls up in front of the house. JUDE *gets out, jumps*
into back with DARKLY.

JUDE (*softly to* DARKLY): You alright, man? Hang in there.
    (*He looks around and calls.*) Callie! Callie! Callie!
    No response. DARKLY *mumbles, still delirious.* JUDE *looks*
    down at him. Then ...

CALLIE (*off*): Jude ...

> JUDE *looks up and sees* CALLIE *coming out of the forest. She has a cool, melancholy beauty: completely self-contained and assured. A blonde, snow-princess, lost within the secretive distance of herself. She's dressed in jeans and white shirt. But she'd look beautiful in anything.*

CALLIE: There's a storm coming.

JUDE: Callie, come over here! Quick!

> CALLIE *rushes to the back of the truck and kneels beside* DARKLY.

CALLIE: What happened?

JUDE: I don't know. He was just laying in the road about a mile or so back.

> CALLIE *feels* DARKLY's *forehead.*

JUDE: What shall we do?

CALLIE: Let's get him in the house.

> JUDE *goes to pick up* DARKLY, *then hesitates.*

JUDE: Clay not here?

> CALLIE *shoots* JUDE *a look, but does not respond.*

INT. CALLIE'S HOMESTEAD, BEDROOM. DAY

Everything is very simple: old wardrobe, bed, chest of drawers. The walls are pale, almost white.

> CALLIE *and* JUDE *lay* DARKLY *on the bed.* CALLIE *starts loosening* DARKLY's *clothes.*

JUDE: I asked you if Clay's gone for one of his walks again.

CALLIE: Just take off his shoes.

JUDE: How long Clay been gone this time? One day? Two?

CALLIE (*holding* DARKLY's *hand*): He looks like he's walked around the world.

JUDE: Callie?

> DARKLY *clutches* CALLIE's *hand, his eyes click open.*

83

CALLIE *and* DARKLY *stare at each other.* DARKLY's *eyes are full of rising panic.*

CALLIE (*gently*): It's alright. You're safe now ... I'll look after you. Just rest. Rest.

The panic in DARKLY's *eyes diminishes. His eyes close.*

JUDE (*still pursuing his own line of thoughts*): Perhaps Clay's gone for good. Living out here driven him mad once and for all.

CALLIE (*flatly at* JUDE): You best start loading the truck. You'll have to do it by yourself today. Clay's been gone two days.

EXT. CALLIE'S HOMESTEAD. DAY

The truck is now parked outside the barn. JUDE *is just loading the final coffin onto the truck.* CALLIE *comes out of the main house.*

JUDE: How's the patient?

CALLIE: Just needs some rest and some food.

CALLIE *watches* JUDE *in silence for a while. Then ...*

CALLIE: I wish you wouldn't joke about it, Jude.

JUDE: Joke about what?

CALLIE: Clay not coming back.

JUDE: Oh, I didn't mean anything by it –

CALLIE: Clay loves me.

JUDE: I know.

CALLIE: He'll come back.

JUDE: Always does ... And, hey, when he does, I've got that tool he ordered.

JUDE *gets large chisel-like tool from back of truck.*

CALLIE: Just put it in the barn.

JUDE: In the barn! Okay!

JUDE *takes the new tool into barn, then returns to the truck.*

84

JUDE: Let me give you the rest of the supplies.

>JUDE *takes supplies from the front seat of truck and hands them to* CALLIE.

JUDE: Now you should come to town to get them, you know.

CALLIE: Give everyone the satisfaction of staring at me. Whispering and judging. I can live without that. Besides, I've got you to fetch things for me.

JUDE: I might not always be here to get them, Callie.

CALLIE: Oh, that's right ... you're going to get away.

JUDE: That's right.

CALLIE (*smiling*): You've been saying that for as long as I've known you.

JUDE: I know.

CALLIE: I bet you'll still be saying it when you're sixty.

JUDE: I want to be a writer.

CALLIE: I'm sure you'll tell wonderful stories.

JUDE: Not living here I won't. Nothing ever happens to tell stories about. Just ... the trees, the truck. Does the truck perceive the tree? Does the tree perceive the truck?

CALLIE: At least you've got a job. Anyone to do with coffins is thriving. One of God's little jokes.

JUDE: Does God play jokes?

CALLIE: All the time.

>JUDE *smiles, considering this. Sound of distant thunder.*

CALLIE: Best get going before the storm sets in.

JUDE: What shall I do about ... (*Indicates house.*)

CALLIE: Leave him.

JUDE: Leave him!

CALLIE: Why not?

JUDE: He might be a criminal or something.

CALLIE: I suppose he might. That's just a chance I'll have to take.

JUDE: But –

CALLIE: They won't look after him properly in town. I know they won't. He's better off here. Really, Jude. Don't worry.

JUDE: Nursed by you! Worth getting exhaustion for any day.

CALLIE: Get out of here.

CALLIE gives him an affectionate kiss on the cheek. JUDE gets in the truck and starts the engine.

JUDE: Take care of yourself, Callie.

CALLIE: You too, Jude. Give my love to Quincy.

JUDE: Sure. See you soon.

CALLIE: Hey, why don't you bring Quincy with you next time.

JUDE: Your wish is my command.

The truck drives away. CALLIE watches it disappear. A flash of lightning. It starts to rain.

INT. CALLIE'S HOMESTEAD, BEDROOM. NIGHT

DARKLY is in bed, calmer and cleaner than before.

CALLIE enters. She's damp from a shower, hair wet, slip clinging to her. DARKLY's clothes are on a chair and CALLIE starts sorting through them. She feels something in the jacket pocket and, after a struggle, gets it out. It is a Bible: the cover is white with silver lettering. CALLIE opens it. On the front page she sees a handwritten name: DARKLY NOON.

CALLIE flicks through the Bible. She finds a photograph. It is of a middle-aged man and woman; very sombre and severely dressed in neat suits, staring straight at the camera. A puritanical nightmare of right wing, religious America.

There is the sound of distant thunder and the electric lights flicker.

DARKLY (*mumbling in his sleep*): . . . came from the top of the mountain . . .

87

CALLIE *goes to the window and looks out. The rain is still torrential.* CALLIE *sits on the edge of the mattress and gently squeezes* DARKLY's *hand.*

CALLIE: Shush now ... It's alright.

EXT. CALLIE'S HOMESTEAD. NIGHT
Rain lashes the homestead!

Thunder!
Lightning!
Darkness!
Lightning!
Darkness!
Light!
Dark ...

Second Day

INT. CALLIE'S HOMESTEAD, BEDROOM. AFTERNOON
DARKLY *is waking up in bed. He looks much better now, stronger. The fever has completely subsided. Sunlight comes through the window.*

Bewildered, DARKLY *looks round the room. He gets out of bed, then realises he's naked. He clutches at the sheet and holds it around him. He looks out of the window and sees –*

INT/EXT. CALLIE'S BEDROOM WINDOW, BARN OUTSIDE.
DAY
– The sun glints on the silvery roof of the barn.

INT. CALLIE'S HOMESTEAD, BEDROOM. DAY
DARKLY *walks away from window. He looks round the room. It's obviously for a couple, man and woman. He goes over to the*

89

wardrobe. Takes out a long coat and puts it on.

   Tentatively – still a little uncertain of his feet – he leaves ...

INT. CALLIE'S HOMESTEAD, STAIRS. AFTERNOON
DARKLY *is walking downstairs. He clutches at the bannister for support. He looks around. The steps creak ominously ...*

EXT. CALLIE'S HOMESTEAD, PORCH. DAY
DARKLY *comes tentatively out of the house. He looks around at the empty courtyard. Then suddenly a noise. Creaking!*

   DARKLY *turns and sees ...* CALLIE *asleep on the swing-chair. She looks so calm, so peaceful, radiant.* DARKLY *is immediately transfixed. At first, too transfixed to move. Then gradually, he starts to approach her.* CALLIE *does not wake.* DARKLY *gets closer and closer, staring at her in wonder.*

   Then, as he stands right above her, she wakes.

CALLIE: You scared me.

DARKLY: I'm sorry.

CALLIE: You shouldn't be up. Really. You should be resting still.

DARKLY: Wh ... where am I?

CALLIE: This is my home. My name's Callie.

INT. CALLIE'S HOMESTEAD, MAIN ROOM. DAY
DARKLY *is sitting at the table, watching as* CALLIE *prepares some food.*

CALLIE: I live here with Clay. The love of my life so to speak. He's a carpenter. Made most everything in the house. He makes coffins. For the undertaker in town ... Clay gets in these moods. He goes for walks. A walk in the dark he calls them. He thinks. Sorts out his

90

problems. He'll be back soon enough. Everything will be alright.

CALLIE *puts a plate of food and a glass of orange juice in front of him.*

CALLIE: Hope you like it.

CALLIE *sits at the table eating a peach, she hears something and looks up.* DARKLY, *despite his hunger, is praying.* CALLIE *watches him.* DARKLY *finishes the prayer, then looks at* CALLIE.

DARKLY: Amen!

CALLIE *has a moment's hesitation before ...*

CALLIE: Oh ... Amen. Of course.

INT. CALLIE'S HOMESTEAD, BEDROOM. DAY

CALLIE *is sorting out some clothes for* DARKLY *to wear.*
DARKLY *sits on bed.*

CALLIE: I had to burn your clothes. They were ruined. I'll find you something of Clay's to wear.

DARKLY: Did you find a Bible in my pocket?

CALLIE: Oh yes! I didn't burn that. I've got it.

CALLIE *gets Bible from sideboard. She looks at the inscription on the front page.*

CALLIE: Darkly Noon. What's that?

DARKLY: Me.

CALLIE: It's your name?

DARKLY: Yes.

CALLIE: That's ... well that's a very peculiar name, isn't it?

DARKLY: Ma and Pa chose it. They stuck a pin in the Bible. It struck the word darkly. You know the passage. Second Corinthians: 13,12. 'For now we see each other through a glass darkly ...'

CALLIE: That's a primitive way to choose a name, isn't it?

91

DARKLY: It's the way we choose our names. It's what we believe.

CALLIE: We?

DARKLY: My people.

CALLIE: Your people. You belong to some kind of sect or cult?

DARKLY: It's not a cult. It's the way it should be. We live by the Bible. All truth is in the Bible.

CALLIE *stares for a moment, weighing up her response. Then she takes photograph from the Bible.*

CALLIE: These your parents?

DARKLY: Yes.

CALLIE: Well, we'd best be giving them a call. I'm sure they're worried about you.

DARKLY: I can't ... They've gone to ... h ... heaven.

CALLIE: Oh, I'm sorry ... what happened to them?

DARKLY: We lived in this s ... small town ... miles from here. Me and my Ma and my Pa ... a whole c ... community of people who believe in the Bible ... The towns-people ... they didn't like us because ... er ...

CALLIE: Because you were different.

DARKLY: The police came. They told us we c ... can't stay there anymore. We have to leave, we can't live the way we want to ... The town p ... people came too ... And then they surrounded us. They were screaming at us all the t ... time. Calling us names ... Doing everything they c ... can to make us surrender ... but we w ... won't change to please them ... They c ... cut off our food. Power. Water. There's helicopters circling overhead all day and n ... night. But it's them who are wrong. They're the heretics! God's on our side. And then one n ... night ... there's an explosion! Fire! Gunshots! ... They attacked us ... I saw my parents get killed. They were shot ... somehow I got away ... Afterwards I just st ... started walking. Just walking

and walking. Didn't know where I was going ... Now
I've got n ... nowhere.

CALLIE: Don't talk like that. Your walking brought you
here. You have this place now. You hear me?

DARKLY: ... Yes.

CALLIE: And you can stay as long as you please.

EXT. ESTABLISHER OF BARN. DAY
Sunlight glints on the silver roof of the barn.

INT. BARN, LOFT AREA. DAY
There's a single bed, a table. Everything sparse and simple.

CALLIE *is showing the place to* DARKLY. DARKLY *is now
dressed in some of* CLAY's *clothes.*

CALLIE: I'm sure you'll be comfortable here. You know ...
I used to stay up here once myself.

DARKLY: Here's fine.

CALLIE: Are you sure?

DARKLY: Very.

CALLIE: Well ... I guess I'll see you in the morning. Sleep
well.

CALLIE *begins going down the ladder.*

CALLIE: If you do need anything, let me know, okay?

DARKLY: Mmm.

DARKLY *sits on the bed. Suddenly he looks very lost, like
a child. With a pitiful sigh, he buries his face in his
hands ...*

93

Third Day

EXT. FOREST. DAY
Golden sunlight shimmers through the forest.
Birds singing.
Insects chirping.
In the distance, the sound of hammering.

EXT. CALLIE'S HOMESTEAD. DAY
The hammering gets louder ...
CALLIE *is on the porch roof, mending a loose slate. The hammer she's violently wielding is at odds with the delicate way she is dressed.* DARKLY *comes out of the barn. He stares at* CALLIE. *Slowly, as if hypnotised by the sight,* DARKLY *approaches the main homestead.* CALLIE *continues to hammer.* DARKLY *stares, approaching.*
Hammering ...
Approaching ...
Hammering ...
Approaching ...
Hammer! Hammer! Hammer!
Finally, DARKLY *comes to a halt. He stares, silently.*
Watching!
Hammering!
Watching!
Hammering ... hammering ... hammering ...
Then –

DARKLY: I ... I could do that.
    CALLIE *is startled by* DARKLY's *cry. She looks down, gives him a surprised smile.*
CALLIE: Sure you're up to it?
DARKLY: Oh ... yeah.
    CALLIE *climbs down a ladder.* DARKLY *helps her and,*

*accidentally, touches her breasts. He jumps back as if he's
got an electric shock.*

DARKLY: I'm sorry, ma'am.

CALLIE: For what?

DARKLY: For ...

CALLIE (*realising*): Oh, that! It's nothing.

DARKLY: But –

CALLIE: Honestly, it's alright, Lee.

DARKLY: Lee?

CALLIE: Yeah ... I've been thinking. I can't call you
Darkly. I'm sorry, but I can't. Lee's alright ain't it?

DARKLY *just stares.* CALLIE *smiles. She takes silence as
consent. She steps up onto porch ...*

CALLIE (*glancing at roof*): Be careful up there. The whole
thing's falling to pieces. Whole damn house'll fall down
one day, I swear it will.

CALLIE *goes into the house. The door slams behind her
violently ...*

INT. CALLIE'S HOMESTEAD, KITCHEN. DAY

CALLIE *is sitting at the table shelling peas.* DARKLY *comes in
from mending the roof. He's dripping with sweat, as proud as a
child after winning a race. And eagerly expecting due praise ...*

CALLIE: Well, thank you very much, kind sir.

DARKLY *smiles very wide.* CALLIE *puts sugar in
saucepan of peas.*

DARKLY: You putting sugar in the peas!

CALLIE: Always have done.

DARKLY: It sh ... should be s ... s ... salt!

CALLIE: Now who laid down that rule?

DARKLY: M ... Ma and Pa.

DARKLY *looks on, confused.* CALLIE *glances up, notices
his expression.*

CALLIE: Lee, I want to talk to you for a second. Come here.
> DARKLY *sits at table.*

CALLIE: Your Ma and Pa ... Your name, and the Bible and ... this cult –

DARKLY: It was the word of God!

CALLIE: Well, sure. But ... what you've got to realise is that ... well ...

DARKLY: G ... God is everywhere!

CALLIE: But not everyone worships God with the same ... how can I say? The same ... harshness as your Ma and Pa.
> DARKLY *frowns, not getting it.*

DARKLY: It's the truth.

CALLIE: Well, surely God meant us to enjoy ourselves. To be happy. To ... just love.
> DARKLY *remains frowning.*

CALLIE: I mean, that's not a sin, is it?
> *Frowning. Silence.*

CALLIE: I mean, I love Clay. May God strike me down if there's something wrong with that –
> *A rifle shot!*

> CALLIE *and* DARKLY *jump!* CALLIE *grabs a rifle by the door and rushes out of the house.* DARKLY *follows ...*

EXT. CALLIE'S HOMESTEAD. DAY
CALLIE *rushes out of the house, followed by* DARKLY.

CALLIE (*loading a rifle*): Leave me alone! You hear me?
> *Another rifle shot.*
>> *Dust erupts!*

CALLIE (*at* DARKLY): It's alright.

DARKLY: B ... but ...
> *Bang!*

*Another rifle shot. The bullet hits the porch. Wood
splinters.*

CALLIE: Jesus! You're going to kill someone one of these
days!

   CALLIE *shoots blindly into the forest.*

CALLIE: You don't scare me! Come out into the open and
shoot!

   CALLIE *shoots again.*

DARKLY (*panicking*): G ... get down!

CALLIE: I'm safe. It's not meant to hurt me, just to let me
know ... (*Angrily back at forest, firing rifle at the trees.*)
... you're out there! Well I know you're out there!
Leave me alone! Let us live in peace. We're not hurting
anyone. You hear me!

   Bang!

      Bang!

      Bang!

CALLIE (*yelling*): We're not hurting anyone! We're not
hurting anyone!

   CALLIE's *rifle runs out of the bullets. The bullets stop
coming out of the forest.*

   Silence.

   Birds singing.

   Insects chirping.

   Long pause.

   CALLIE, *exhausted, returns to the house.*

DARKLY: Who was that? Was that Clay?

CALLIE (*angrily*): Of course it wasn't Clay. Why would
Clay shoot at me? (*Calms down.*) No. It wasn't Clay.
Don't worry about it. It won't happen again for a
while.

EXT. ESTABLISHING SHOT, CALLIE'S HOMESTEAD. NIGHT
The trees of the forest seem like vast sentinels around the house.
Icy blue moonlight shimmers on the silver roof of the house.
Insects ...

INT. CALLIE'S HOMESTEAD, KITCHEN. NIGHT
CALLIE *and* DARKLY *have just finished eating.* CALLIE *is*
trying to find a station on the radio. DARKLY *watches her.*
CALLIE *notices his look.*

CALLIE: Give me a smile.

> DARKLY *manages a smile.*

CALLIE: That's better ... (*She resumes fiddling with radio.*)
Oh, only Clay can get this radio to work.

> DARKLY *sighs deeply. He wants to talk to her, to engage*
> *with her in some way. But she is as beyond him as he is*
> *distanced from her.*

CALLIE: Oh, Clay! Clay! Come home.

DARKLY (*standing*): G ... goodnight.

CALLIE: Oh, you don't have to go. Stay a while longer. Talk
to me. Tell me things about, you know, how you lived
and everything.

DARKLY (*flatly*): No.

EXT. CALLIE'S HOMESTEAD. NIGHT
DARKLY *leaves the house. He walks towards the barn.*

INT./EXT. THE BARN, LOFT. NIGHT
DARKLY *is sitting on the bed. His face is tense, jaws clenched.*
Trying to work a problem out, not even sure exactly what the
problem is.

> *Then –* CALLIE *comes out of main house. She lights a*

98

cigarette. From where he's sitting, DARKLY can see her. He watches, transfixed ...

CALLIE (*sighing*): Clay! ... Clay!
>   DARKLY *continues to watch. Jaws clench tighter.*
>   *Tense ...*

CALLIE (*half call, half sigh*): Clay ... ! Oh, come back home, Clay.
>   CALLIE *looks up and sees* DARKLY.

CALLIE: You alright, Lee?

DARKLY: Yeah.
>   *They stare at each other for a moment.*

DARKLY: You shouldn't smoke.

CALLIE: Why?

DARKLY: It's a sin.
>   *Pause.*
>   >   *They stare.*
>   >   *Insects ...*

CALLIE: Goodnight, Lee.
>   CALLIE *goes into the house. The fly door slams violently shut once more ...*

Fourth Day

EXT. CALLIE'S HOMESTEAD. DAY
Dazzling sunlight shimmers on the white and silver of the house. The trees, magnificent and green, dwarf everything.
>   *Birds sing.*
>   *Insects chirp.*

INT. CALLIE'S HOMESTEAD, KITCHEN. DAY
CALLIE *is standing by the window, sipping lemonade.*
DARKLY, *also drinking lemonade, stands nearby, watching. Ice*

99

tinkles in glasses. CALLIE *takes ice cube from glass. She runs it over her chest, cooling herself. She looks at* DARKLY *and smiles. He tries to smile back, but can't quite manage it. She sips more lemonade.*

Ice tinkles.

Insects ...

Tinkle ...

Sip.

Tinkle ...

CALLIE: It's so hot today.

DARKLY *nods, his eyes glued to her.*

Tinkle ... tinkle ... tinkle ...

CALLIE: I have an idea.

CALLIE *starts to leave the room.* DARKLY *frowns.*

DARKLY: Wh ... what?

CALLIE: Come on.

DARKLY *hesitates.*

CALLIE (*firmer*): Come on!

EXT. THE FOREST, A HOT SPA. DAY

CALLIE *and* DARKLY *approaching spa,* DARKLY *still a little bewildered.*

CALLIE: Look, Lee! It's a spa.

DARKLY: Mmm ...

CALLIE: Let's have a soak.

DARKLY: Wh ... what?

CALLIE *starts to take her clothes off.* DARKLY *watches, transfixed – half wonder, half horror.*

DARKLY: Don't do that!

CALLIE: Why?

DARKLY: You shouldn't.

CALLIE: Being naked isn't the same as sex, you know.

DARKLY: It's a sin.

CALLIE: What? Sex?

DARKLY: That's right.

CALLIE: Don't tell me that's what your Ma and Pa always said.

DARKLY: It's the word of God.

CALLIE *strips to her slip.*

CALLIE: Well, I'll just stay like this. That's not a sin is it?

DARKLY: No.

CALLIE: That's a relief.

CALLIE *gets into spa, splashes around, steam rising.*

DARKLY *stares down.*

CALLIE: Jump in, Lee! There's no one here but you and me.

CALLIE *continues to enjoy herself in the water. She is perfectly content and at ease with the situation.* DARKLY *relaxes a little. He sits down and continues to gaze. For a flickering moment he understands. Yes! This is how it can be! There is no problem.*

CALLIE *splashes water.*

DARKLY *gazes.*

Splashing.

Gazing.

Splashing.

Gazing ... gazing ... gazing ...

Then ...

CALLIE (*feeling her scalp*): There's something in my hair. I think it's an insect. Can you get it out for me?

DARKLY *nods.* CALLIE *gets out of the spa and sits next to* DARKLY. *They are very close.*

CALLIE (*softly*): Can you see it? Careful ...

CALLIE's *breasts are heaving, glistening with droplets. She is pressing against* DARKLY's *chest, making his own shirt wet ... She is breathing heavily.*

CALLIE: Don't hurt it!

CALLIE's *breath is delicate, close to* DARKLY's *ear. He*

swallows. Starts feeling her hair. CALLIE *gasps.* DARKLY
swallows.

CALLIE: Careful!

DARKLY *is half terrified. Half ecstatic. The smell of
her . . .*

CALLIE: Careful . . .

The feel of her . . . Her hair . . . Her wet skin.

CALLIE: Careful . . .

*Finally, he untangles the insect. A dragonfly. He shows it
to* CALLIE. *It's dead.*

DARKLY: I think I killed it.

CALLIE *stares at* DARKLY. DARKLY *stares back.*

*He looks so lost. And, for a brief moment, this is how
they understand each other. The lost talking to the lost.*

CALLIE (*very gently*): I want to show you something.

DARKLY: What?

CALLIE: Follow me.

EXT. FOREST, APPROACH TO CAVE. DAY
CALLIE *and* DARKLY *walk up to entrance of cave . . .*

INT. THE CAVE. DAY
*The cave is very large. As majestic as a cathedral. On the walls
are ancient Indian paintings. One is a blood-red hand print.*

CALLIE: This is my favourite place in the whole world . . .
we're right in the middle of the woods . . . It's heart.

DARKLY: Someone told me you can only walk halfway into a
forest. After that . . . you're walking out.

CALLIE: Well, whoever told you that was wrong. You can
walk as far into the woods as you have a mind to. It can
go on forever sometimes.

CALLIE *touches the blood-red print on the wall.*

102

CALLIE: Did you see this? It's been here for thousands of years. And you know what it's saying ... ? 'I am here'. That's what it's saying. 'I'm part of time. There may be nothing left of me but this hand print. But I'm still part of it.' (*She lays her hand on the hand print.*) I believe. (*Pause.*) I believe.

DARKLY *stares in wonder. He could be a kid in a cave full of treasure ... Gradually, he starts approaching* CALLIE.

DARKLY: Callie ...

CALLIE *looks at* DARKLY.

DARKLY: I've never met anyone like ... like you ...

CALLIE *stares at* DARKLY, *smiling.*

DARKLY: I think about you ...

CALLIE: I know.

DARKLY *is getting closer and closer to* CALLIE, *struggling to say something.* CALLIE *puts him out of his misery –*

CALLIE: I care about you very much. I want you to be part of our family. Please don't spoil anything.

CALLIE *smiles at* DARKLY, *then leaves the cave.*

DARKLY *stares after her ...*

INT. THE BARN, MAIN AREA. NIGHT

DARKLY *is looking for something. He finds a tin box with a few nails inside. He empties the nails from the tin box. They clatter on the ground –*

INT./EXT. THE BARN, LOFT. NIGHT

DARKLY *turns on light and sits at table. The Bible is on table.* DARKLY *puts tin box on table. He takes the photograph of his Ma and Pa from the Bible. He puts the Bible in the tin box, then the photograph. Then ...*

DARKLY *hears the fly door open and close.* DARKLY *stands up and peers through crack ... He sees* CALLIE *sitting on the porch, smoking.* DARKLY *watching; he breathes faster.*

CALLIE *leans back, relaxing.* DARKLY *unbuckles his belt. He unzips his fly. We see his eye peering at* CALLIE *as he ... Reaches in his jeans. Starts feeling himself. He's breathing faster and faster, rasping. He's rubbing himself violently, panting.*

Rasping ...

Panting ...

Staring ...

Rubbing ...

Rasp, pant, stare, rub ...

Rasp, rasp, rasp, rasp ...

Then, suddenly reaching his climax, he cries out as if in pain.

Fifth Day

EXT. CALLIE'S HOMESTEAD, NEARBY AREA WITH FLOWERS. DAY

DARKLY *is picking some flowers. He has the appearance of a love-sick youth now.*

In the distance ... CALLIE *comes out on the porch. She feels the sun against her skin. Enjoys it.*

DARKLY *watches. Picks another flower. Then another. Another ... And then –*

CALLIE *sees something. She cries out with excitement –*

CALLIE: Clay!

Now DARKLY *sees –* CLAY *is approaching the homestead. He is in his late twenties, unshaven, in need of a wash. He has brooding good looks, and a playful, infectious grin.*

CALLIE *runs into his arms. He picks her up, swirls her round, kisses her.*

CALLIE: I knew you'd be back! I just knew it.

CLAY *carries her back towards the house.*

DARKLY's *look has changed. Gone is the love-sick youth. He is glaring at them. He is crushing the flowers in his hands.*

CALLIE *and* CLAY *disappear inside the house.*

DARKLY *looks down ... He sees something glistening at his feet. Carefully, he picks it up. It is the size of a small bird and made out of barbed wire. The barbed wire has been rolled into a ball and is decorated with a few feathers.*

DARKLY *stares at the barbed wire bird and frowns. Although he's been holding it gently, the barbed wire has pricked his finger.*

CALLIE *rushes back out onto the porch.*

CALLIE: Lee! Lee! Where are you? Come home!

DARKLY *sucks blood from his finger ...*

CALLIE: Lee!

Blood!

CALLIE: Lee!

Blood!

INT. CALLIE'S HOMESTEAD, KITCHEN. NIGHT

CALLIE, CLAY *and* DARKLY *are sitting round the table. They've just finished eating.* CALLIE *is nibbling at an apple. The light bulb above the table flashes and crackles.* CALLIE *and* CLAY *look at each other and laugh.*

CALLIE: Everything's falling apart. Clay's the only one who can fix anything round here.

CLAY *makes a clucking sound at the back of his throat.*

CALLIE: I said he can stay here, Clay. Say he can. Oh, he can, can't he? Say yes.

Cluck!

DARKLY: How come he can't talk?

CALLIE *finishes the apple, puts core on the table.*

106

CALLIE: Born that way. Still, he don't need words.

> *Cluck! Cluck!*
>
> *Playfully,* CLAY *runs his fingers through* CALLIE's *hair. As if by magic, he produces a feather.*
>
> *Cluck! Cluck!*
>
> CALLIE *giggles and puts it behind her ear. Now* CLAY *is looking down the front of* CALLIE's *dress.*
>
> *Cluck! Whistle! Cluck!*
>
> DARKLY *is looking on, embarassed.* CLAY *finds a wood cone between* CALLIE's *breasts.*
>
> *Whistle!*
>
> *Again, she laughs, and puts it on the table.* CLAY *is searching again ... behind her ear this time. He finds a tiny, blue egg.*
>
> *Cluck! Whistle!*
>
> CALLIE *looks at the egg, her smile diminishing. She puts the egg on the table.*

CALLIE: That's enough. Clay.

> CLAY *looks upset. Cluck?*

CALLIE: Lee has no-one, Clay. His parents were killed in a terrible accident. He's got no-one ... but us. We can look after him. We can be his new family.

> CLAY *becomes serious. Whistle! He looks at* DARKLY, *then 'clucks' his approval.*

CALLIE: So he can stay! Oh, Clay, I love you!

> CALLIE *embraces* CLAY. DARKLY *looks at* CALLIE's *hand.*

DARKLY: You're not ... wearing a ring.

CALLIE: No, we're not married.

> CLAY *sweeps* CALLIE *off her feet. He carries her up the stairs.* DARKLY *looks lost: Why would they go upstairs? This is a world beyond him: The language of another planet! He's never felt so alien ...*

CALLIE: Goodnight, Lee.

> *Cluck!*

DARKLY *sits alone for a while. He looks at the apple core on the table. Then ... he picks up the apple core and leaves.*

EXT. CALLIE'S HOMSTEAD. NIGHT
DARKLY *walks out of the house and goes towards the barn ...*

INT. BARN, LOFT AREA. NIGHT
DARKLY *picks up tin box from table, then sits on bed. He opens the tin box. Inside it is the Bible. The photograph of his parents ... And the barbed wire bird. Now* DARKLY *puts the apple core in the box. He studies the contents for a few moments, then closes the lid.*

DARKLY *falls to the mattress. He's in great pain. He sobs gently.*

Sixth Day

EXT. THE FOREST. DAY
Sun rays stab through the branches.
   Birds!
   Insects.

INT. THE BARN, MAIN AREA. DAY
DARKLY *and* CLAY *are both working;* DARKLY *sandpapering a cradle,* CLAY *shaving the bark (with the large chisel-tool* JUDE *had brought earlier) from some wood.* DARKLY *is watching* CLAY. *He wants to ask something, but is finding it difficult to pluck up the courage. Finally, he manages ...*

DARKLY: Have you loved Callie ... ?
   CLAY *keeps on working, not listening.*

DARKLY (*louder*): How long you loved Callie . . . ? A long time?

> CLAY *indicates* DARKLY *should continue with his work. And* DARKLY *does . . . for a while. But then –*

DARKLY: Hey . . . have you ever considered getting married?

> CLAY *clucks impatiently.*

DARKLY: You could make it right in the eyes of God and . . . and . . . and . . .

> *Cluck!*

>> DARKLY *pauses, stares.* CLAY *once more indicating* DARKLY *should continue his work . . .*

DARKLY: But –

> *Cluck!*

DARKLY: But –

> *CLUCK! CLUCK!*

>> DARKLY *resumes work . . .*

EXT. CALLIE'S HOMESTEAD, BARN. NIGHT
Moonlight gleams on the silver roof.

INT. THE BARN, LOFT AREA. NIGHT
DARKLY *is praying.*

DARKLY (*mumbling*): Ma . . . Pa . . . what shall I do? Help me . . . Show me the way . . .

> *We continue hearing his prayer, but cut to . . .*

EXT. THE FOREST. NIGHT
The wind moving like a living thing through the trees. The very forest seems to be alive with invisible monsters . . .

DARKLY (*voice over*): What shall I do? Ma! Pa! Help me.

INT. THE BARN, LOFT AREA. NIGHT

DARKLY: Amen.

Seventh Day

EXT. CALLIE'S HOMESTEAD. DAY
*The sun is scorchingly hot, blazing down on the homestead and
barn.* DARKLY *is sandpapering a coffin propped against the
barn doorway.* CLAY *comes out of the barn, lighting a cigarette.
He sits down on seat.*
   Whistle!
   DARKLY *looks.*
   Cluck! Cluck! Cluck!
   CLAY *slaps seat. He wants* DARKLY *to sit next to him.*

DARKLY: But I've g ... got work to –
   Cluck!
      Reluctantly, DARKLY *sits.* CLAY *mimes something: he
   wants to know if* DARKLY *has a coin.*
DARKLY: I d ... don't have any money.
   Cluck!
      CLAY *searches his own pocket. Finds a coin. And shows*
   DARKLY *a trick with it.* DARKLY *is not impressed.*
   CALLIE *comes out of the house and stands on the porch,
   watching. She is content – happy her 'new family' seem to
   be getting on so well.* CLAY, *meanwhile, is trying to get*
   DARKLY *to try the trick with the coin.* DARKLY *doesn't
   want to. He's obviously getting irritated by* CLAY *now.*
   CLAY *perseveres. Cluck! Cluck! Cluck!* DARKLY
   snatches his hand away.
DARKLY: No!
   Then we hear something ...
QUINCY (*voice over*): Hallelujah! Hallelujah!
   CALLIE *sees the Chevrolet truck approaching.*
   110

CALLIE: Hey! It looks like Quincy's come with Jude.

The truck comes to a halt in front of the homestead.

QUINCY and JUDE get out. QUINCY is dressed in sombre black, despite the heat. He is a large 'theatrical' character, mopping his brow with a white handkerchief. He's the undertaker we'd heard mentioned earlier.

CALLIE: Quincy! Good to see you!

QUINCY: Just keeps getting hotter, doesn't it, my dear? People are dropping like flies. I bring orders for coffins. Money jangles in my pockets. Hope you're well, Callie?

CALLIE: You get worse as you get older, Quincy. (*They kiss.*) And I'm fine. How you doing, Jude?

JUDE: Fine.

CALLIE: Have you looked behind you?

CLAY has crept up behind JUDE. JUDE turns to see him.

JUDE: Hey! Nature boy.

CALLIE: Told you he'd be back.

JUDE: I didn't doubt it. How are you, Clay?

Cluck!

CALLIE: And ... as you can see, your good deed worked out just fine. Lee! This here's Jude. He's the one who found you.

DARKLY: Thanks for helping me.

JUDE: It was nothing. You feeling better?

DARKLY: I ... I ... I ...

CALLIE: Yes! He's doing just great. Been helping Clay ...

JUDE (*at CLAY*): With ... ?

Cluck: mimes hammering.

JUDE: Really! Any good?

Cluck!

CALLIE: Quincy!

QUINCY is in a world of his own, mopping his brow.

CALLIE: Quincy! You listening to me, you old devil.

QUINCY: That's the second time you've called me old, young lady. I'll have you know you're as young as you feel and I feel like a baby. I'm a baby of death. Corpses keep me juvenile. Misery is money. And grief ... well, that's a miracle. (*He goes to* DARKLY.) How do you do, young sir. Jude told me he found a little lost thing on the brink of death. I said, 'The brink's no good. Couldn't you push him all the way?'

CALLIE: Lee, this is Quincy. He's the undertaker.

QUINCY: The Impresario of Undertakers, young lady!

CALLIE, CLAY *and* JUDE *seem to stand back, enjoying* QUINCY's *performance.* DARKLY — *on the other hand — isn't quite sure what he's seeing. He doesn't know whether to laugh or cry.*

QUINCY: I get the dead and scoop out their smelly bits ...

CALLIE: Oh, Quincy ... be quiet —

JUDE: He's started now ...

QUINCY: I stitch them up and package them in overcoats of wood. Made by the wonderful Clay here ...

CALLIE: And Lee!

QUINCY: Of course, of course! I don't charge much. I make dying a luxury. If not a necessity. It's the most economical thing you'll ever do!

CALLIE, CLAY *and* JUDE *are all laughing.*

CALLIE: Come on! Let's get out of the heat.

QUINCY: Okay ... By the way, what do you have in the house to drink. Or *who* do you have?

EXT. CALLIE'S HOMESTEAD. DAY
Sun has set a bit lower now ... Light changed from yellow to amber ...

JUDE *and* DARKLY *are just loading the final coffin onto the truck. On the porch,* CALLIE, CLAY *and* QUINCY *laugh and sip lemonade.*

JUDE: I've been working with Quincy for ... oh, years now. Live with him in the town. He's alright I guess, but – Jesus – I gotta get away. There must be more than collecting coffins and listening to the grieving. You know what I'm saying?

JUDE looks at DARKLY's buttoned-up shirt.

JUDE: You must be burning up in that thing. Why don't you undo a button or something?

JUDE realises DARKLY isn't even listening. DARKLY is looking at the porch. Staring at CALLIE.

JUDE: Hey!

Staring.

   CALLIE sits in CLAY's lap.

   Staring.

   JUDE follows DARKLY's gaze. CALLIE kisses CLAY.

JUDE looks at DARKLY once more ...

JUDE: Hey!

Staring!

JUDE (*louder*): Hey!

DARKLY snaps round.

DARKLY: Wh ... what?

JUDE: Let's talk.

EXT. MOUNTAIN LEDGE. DAY

JUDE and DARKLY stand on ledge, overlooking the forest. The landscape seems to go on forever.

JUDE: You know, Callie's the most beautiful thing in the whole world. She's like the forest. A wild sort of beauty. Like it's always been here. Know what I mean?

DARKLY tries to answer but can't.

JUDE: Sure you know! It's funny! I feel responsible for you in a way.

DARKLY: Wh ... why?

113

JUDE: 'Cos I found you I guess. I mean, I saved your life. Some people'll say that makes me responsible. Well, either way, it was me who brought you here. Into the forest. That's why I'm saying what I'm saying.

DARKLY: I don't ... know ... what –

JUDE: Listen! Callie loves Clay. She has since the first time she saw him. And he's loved her from the first time he saw her. I know what you're feeling. I could see it in your eyes back there.

DARKLY (*angrily*): You're wr ... wrong!

JUDE: Alright, alright ... so I'm wrong. I apologise.

DARKLY (*calming down*): Alright.

JUDE: But just do one thing for me. Even though I'm wrong ... don't forget what I said. Alright? (*Smiles.*) Alright?

Gradually, DARKLY *smiles back.*

JUDE: Hey! Wanna see something?

DARKLY: Sure.

JUDE sits down on the ground.

JUDE: Sit down.

DARKLY doesn't move.

JUDE: Sit down!

DARKLY: I'm fine!

JUDE: Go on! Sit down!

Awkwardly, DARKLY *sits.* JUDE *takes a small pouch from his pocket.*

JUDE (*grinning*): You ready?

DARKLY nods. JUDE *takes a whitish, egg-shaped object from the pouch and holds it up.*

JUDE (*grinning*): You know what this is?

DARKLY: An egg.

JUDE: No. It looks like an egg, but it ain't ... Guess again.

DARKLY: A r ... rock.

JUDE: A rock? No! This here's prehistoric ... fossilised dinosaur shit.

DARKLY: No!

115

JUDE: Brachiosaurus, to be precise. Want to hold it?

DARKLY (*taking fossil*): But there's no such thing.

JUDE: Well, what's this then? Brachiosaurus sat down about a million years ago and shat that ... Don't it feel like dinosaur shit?

DARKLY (*laughing*): I don't know.

JUDE: Hey, why don't you keep it? I want to give it to you as a gift ... You want it?

DARKLY (*laughing*): No!

JUDE: This shit's a national treasure. What you laughing at?

DARKLY: Don't swear.

JUDE: Why you laughing at me? Shit, shit, shit, dinosaur shit.

DARKLY: Don't.

JUDE: Shit!

DARKLY: Don't! Don't!

EXT. CALLIE'S HOMESTEAD. DAY

The sun has set even more. Light changed from amber to red.
QUINCY *is just leaving. He approaches the truck with*
CALLIE *and* DARKLY *and* JUDE. CLAY *sits on the porch.*

QUINCY: You heal the sick, Callie. That's no good to me. I'd be out of business in a week if everyone was like you. Everywhere else people are starving to death. Dropping like flies. Nobody has any money, no job. Nothing. People begging for food. It's the end of the world! Hallelujah!

CALLIE: You sound like a preacher again, Quincy.

QUINCY: My pa was a preacher. I tell you that?

CALLIE: A million times!

QUINCY: He taught me how to preach. You know what he said, 'Begin slow and very low, then get higher till you catch fire!' I believe that too. That's what I do. It's the end of the world! Hallelujah! Money jangles, money jangles. Hallelujah! Hallelujah! It's the end of the world! Hallelujah!

CALLIE: Just go, Quincy. Before you talk us all six foot under.

QUINCY: Now there's an idea.

CALLIE embraces QUINCY and he gets into the truck.
JUDE smiles at DARKLY, then he too gets in and starts the engine.

JUDE (*at DARKLY*): Hey, I'll visit you soon, okay?

DARKLY: Good.

The truck drives away.

QUINCY (*his voice fading*): It's the end of the world! Hallelujah! Hallelujah!

It's the end of the world.

It's the end of the world.

It's the end of the world.

INT./EXT. THE BARN, LOFT AREA. NIGHT

DARKLY *is in loft of barn. In the distance, we can hear the sound of CALLIE and CLAY making love. They're groaning.*

DARKLY is very disturbed. He is sobbing with pain.

Groan! ...

Sob! ...

Groan! ...

To escape the noise, DARKLY rushes out of barn and into –

EXT. THE FOREST. NIGHT

DARKLY *walks through the forest. It is so calm. Peaceful. His footsteps crunch on leaves. Owls hoot. Insects.*

The forest is like another world. A world DARKLY feels safe in ...

Eighth Day

EXT. THE FOREST, RIVER. DAY

DARKLY *is asleep by a river. He's obviously spent the night there. Leaves and morning dew cling to him.*

Suddenly . . . Light sparkles on his face. A twinkling, magical light, more intense than just sunlight on water.

DARKLY*'s eyes flutter open. He sees something. Stares in bewilderment for a while. Then sits. He stares a moment longer. The glistening light is still on his face. We don't know what he's staring at yet. But – whatever it is – it makes him stand . . .*

DARKLY *stares in wonder. The light sparkling on him grows more intense. And, then, we see what he's looking at . . . A giant silver shoe is floating down the river. It glistens and twinkles in the sunlight.*

DARKLY *follows the silver shoe with his eyes. It serenely floats downriver. It hardly causes a ripple on the mirror-like surface of the water.* DARKLY*'s confused by the sight, yet hypnotised by it, captivated.*

Sparkling.

Twinkling.

Floating.

Staring.

Gradually, the silver shoe floats out of sight . . .

EXT. THE FOREST. DAY

DARKLY *walks through the forest. There is something trance-like about him now. As if trapped in wondrous shock. The sight of the silver shoe has touched him in some way. Unlocked something, some loss of sanity. He continues walking and then –*

118

EXT. THE FOREST, BY THE FALLEN TREE. DAY

– he hears barking. A DOG *is rushing at him.*

DARKLY *jumps back.*

The DOG *is dark, very old, but still vicious as a clenched fist. It comes to rest in front of* DARKLY, *barking, barking.*

A woman appears out of the undergrowth, holding a gun. She is wearing old work clothes, has unkempt hair and the kind of chiselled hardness that can only come from a once strikingly beautiful face. She's about fifty years old. Her name is ROXY.

ROXY (*indicating the* DOG): Don't be scared. She won't hurt you.

Bark! Bark!

DARKLY *freezes.* ROXY *casually strolls up.*

ROXY: Well, just so long as you don't make any sudden movements.

Bark! Bark!

ROXY *prowls round* DARKLY, *staring at him.*

DARKLY, *for his part, doesn't take his eyes off the* DOG.

ROXY: Seems to me like you spent the whole night in this forest.

DARKLY: I ... I did.

Bark! Bark!

EXT. THE FOREST, PATH TO ROXY'S HOME. DAY

ROXY *is walking through the forest, the* DOG *at her feet.* DARKLY *follows.*

ROXY: Don't need people. Not anymore. People let you down. You love them, give them everything. And then they leave you. The forest is all I need now.

DARKLY: ... It's beautiful here.

ROXY: Beautiful! (*Pause.*) Well, no, come to think of it I used to feel the same way but you can't let that fool you,

119

boy. Don't you know how a thing can be beautiful on top and underneath it's uglier than sin. (*Pause.*) That's because of the monster.

DARKLY: ... What monster?

ROXY: What ... ? Oh, the monster of the forest, boy. It's out there. Vicious, mean, spiteful. Teeth like knives. And you know what it feeds on.

DARKLY: What?

ROXY: Men! Beautiful young men. Men just like you.

DARKLY: Have you seen it?

ROXY: Oh, yeah. I've seen it. (*She points.*) That's where I live, boy.

EXT. THE FOREST, OUTSIDE ROXY'S SILVER BULLET. DAY
A silver mobile home – commonly known as a Silver Bullet – gleams in a small clearing. It has a bizarre, surreal appearance, almost like an abandoned flying-saucer in the undergrowth.
  ROXY *approaches the home, the* DOG *scurrying at her feet.*

ROXY: My name's Roxy, by the way. Just Roxy and her dog ... (*Pats* DOG *affectionately.*) ... That's me.
  DARKLY *follows* ROXY. *Suddenly, he sees something in the undergrowth. He picks it up.*

DARKLY: I found ... I found one of these.
  It's another one of the birds made of barbed wire and feathers. It glints spitefully in the sunlight.

ROXY: Careful! That's the barbed wire.

DARKLY: Barbed wire?

ROXY: Yeah. There must be lots of those all over the forest.

DARKLY: ... Why?

ROXY: I used them to train Dog here. See when I shoot a bird, Dog has to go and get them. In the early days Dog used to bite down. Used to turn them to a pulp. So, made that! When she went to retrieve it, that thing, and

bit down – boy did she know it! Had to be done though.
Gave her a soft mouth ... Let's get in the house.

DARKLY *and* ROXY *go into* ROXY'*s mobile home.*

INT. ROXY'S SILVER BULLET. DAY

DARKLY *and* ROXY *enter ... It's simply furnished, clean and
tidy.*

ROXY: Wanna sit down?

DARKLY: Mmm.

ROXY (*looking round*): Well, what do you think?

DARKLY: It's very ...

DARKLY'*s voice fades away.*

ROXY: Well, it's home. *My* home. That's the important
thing. I've got a roof over my head and food to eat.
These days, that's a minor miracle. (*Slight pause.*) It's
like the Dark Ages. Nobody cares anymore. Nobody
cares for the family –

DARKLY: You're absolutely right.

ROXY: You got a family?

A deep sadness ripples through DARKLY.

DARKLY: I had one.

ROXY *responds to this sadness. There's a beat before she
responds with ...*

ROXY: Stay and have some coffee with me.

DARKLY: No. I've got to get back –

ROXY (*suddenly harsh*): To her?

DARKLY *stares at* ROXY.

DARKLY: I ... wh ...

ROXY: I know where you're staying!

DARKLY: W ... with Callie.

ROXY: That's what she calls herself. But you know who she
is really.

DARKLY: Who?

121

ROXY: Witch!

DARKLY: Why?

ROXY: Why? That's what she is so that's her name. And if you're staying with her but sleeping out in the forest I think you know that. Her name's witch, boy! She's a witch!

INT. CALLIE'S HOMESTEAD, KITCHEN. DAY

CALLIE *is sitting on sofa, cleaning rifle.* DARKLY *enters ...*

CALLIE: There you are. I was beginning to worry. (*Slight pause.*) I thought you might have gone back to take another look at the cave.

DARKLY: ... No.

CALLIE: What did you do, then? Just go for a walk? You missed breakfast. You want me to fix you something?

DARKLY: ... N ... no.

CALLIE *stares at him, registers his look. Pause.*

CALLIE (*flatly*): You met her.

DARKLY: W ... who?

CALLIE: Don't play games. You went into the forest and you met her. Roxy.

DARKLY: Yes.

CALLIE: What did she tell you?

DARKLY: Not much.

CALLIE: But the little she did was about me, eh?

DARKLY: Mmm.

CALLIE: She call me a witch?

DARKLY: Yeah.

CALLIE: You should ignore her, Lee. You hear me? She's crazy.

DARKLY: She d ... didn't seem –

CALLIE: Well she is! Crazy. Did she say anything else. Apart from calling me a witch?

122

DARKLY: No.

>*Slight pause.*

CALLIE: Stay away from her, Lee. Roxy has ... has her own reasons for hating me.

DARKLY: Like what?

CALLIE: Please don't make me talk about it, Lee. Clay and me, we're happy here. That's really all that matters.

>DARKLY *stares, waiting for more.*

CALLIE: Roxy's a crazy woman. (*Pause.*) Trust me.

INT. BARN, MAIN AREA. DAY

DARKLY *is painting the cradle that he was sandpapering earlier. He's painting it red.*

>*Bright red.*
>*But he looks pre-occupied. Mind not really on the job.*
>*He finishes painting the cradle, then goes to wash his hands.*
>*His hands are red.*
>*Bright red ...*

INT. THE BARN, LOFT AREA. NIGHT

DARKLY *is kneeling in prayer. In front of him is the silver tin box. He opens it ... Inside we see the Bible. The apple core (now rotten). The glossy photograph of his parents. And the barbed wire bird.*

>DARKLY *takes the barbed wire bird from the box. Clutches it between his hands as he prays. He's obviously in great distress. Sweat gleams over his forehead. He's trembling. His praying gets more intense. So does the clutching ...*

>*Blood drips from his hands ... It falls into the open tin box.*
>*Red on silver.*
>*Then onto the Bible.*
>*Red ...*

123

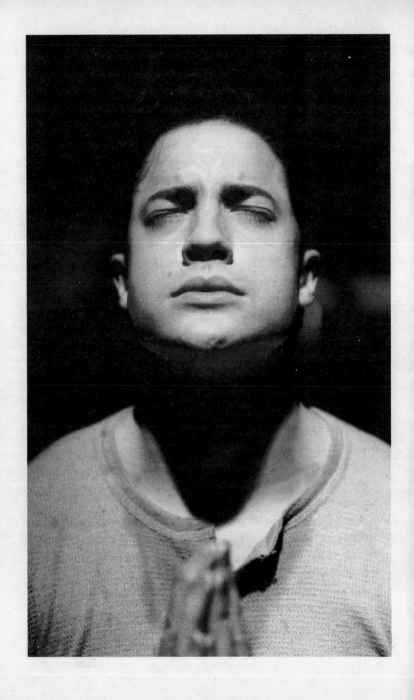

Ninth Day

INT. CALLLIE'S HOMESTEAD, MAIN ROOM. DAY
CALLIE *and* DARKLY *are sitting at the table.* CALLIE *is bandaging* DARKLY*'s hand.*

CALLIE: You should be careful.
    CALLIE *looks at* DARKLY*'s hand.*
      DARKLY *looks at* CALLIE.
      CALLIE *looks up at* DARKLY.
      DARKLY *looks away.*
CALLIE: It can get infected.
    CALLIE *looks at* DARKLY*'s hand.*
      DARKLY *looks at* CALLIE.
      CALLIE *looks up at* DARKLY.
      DARKLY *looks away.*
CALLIE: Turn to poison.
    CALLIE *looks at* DARKLY*'s hand.*
      DARKLY *looks at* CALLIE.
      CALLIE *looks up at* DARKLY.
      DARKLY *looks away.*
CALLIE: You'd be surprised how easy it happens ... How does that feel?
DARKLY: It ... it feels much better.
    CALLIE *looks at* DARKLY*'s hand.*
      DARKLY *looks at* CALLIE.
      CALLIE *looks up at* DARKLY.
      This time, DARKLY *holds his look.*
CALLIE: What?
    DARKLY *continues staring.*
CALLIE: What?
    Finally DARKLY *unlocks his stare. He gets up, leaving.*
CALLIE: You going to help Clay?
DARKLY: N ... no.
    CALLIE *follows him.*

EXT. CALLIE'S HOMESTEAD, THE PORCH. DAY

CALLIE *comes out after* DARKLY *and watches him go into the forest.*

CALLIE (*calling*): Don't be long! (*Pause.*) There's work to do!

> CALLIE *hears a whistle. She turns to see* CLAY *coming out of the barn.* CLAY *indicates* DARKLY, *and looks questioningly at* CALLIE.
>
> *Cluck! Whistle!*

CALLIE: It's nothing ... He'll be back in a while.

> CALLIE *watches* DARKLY *disappear in the forest ...*

EXT. ROXY'S SILVER BULLET. DAY

DARKLY *and* ROXY *are sitting outside* ROXY'S *mobile home. The* DOG *at* ROXY'S *feet. There's a small table between them with a large pitcher of lemonade.*

DARKLY: She said I wasn't supposed to see you again.

ROXY: 'Course she did ... She knows I know what she is, that's why.

DARKLY: A witch.

ROXY: On her good days, yes ... (*Pause.*) There's something I've been wanting to show you ... (*Hands* DARKLY *a small photograph.*) Here!

DARKLY: A photograph?

ROXY: Tell me what you see.

> *The photograph is of a family – a mother, father, a boy of about eight or nine. The child in his mother's embrace, her hand planted firmly on his head, as if holding him down.*

DARKLY: ... A family.

ROXY: My family.

DARKLY: Yours?

ROXY: Years ago.

126

DARKLY: Wh ... what happened?

ROXY: *She* happened.

DARKLY: Callie?

ROXY: The witch happened!

DARKLY: You can tell me about it.

> ROXY *takes a deep breath. She never had any intention not to tell him. She sits back in the chair – her moment has come.*

ROXY: Once, boy, I lived in a house ... That house where you're living now ... I lived there with Jake, my husband there, and my beautiful boy. And then, one day, my husband found a girl on the edge of the forest. She was sorely tired and had a broken ankle. So my husband brought her back to our home – to *my* house! I knew she was evil from the start. She started to tempt him, to tease him ...

> DARKLY *stares at* ROXY *intently. This has touched a very deep and real nerve in him.*

ROXY: She made him lose control. It wasn't his fault. It was her.

DARKLY: Yes! Yes!

ROXY: She killed him!

DARKLY: Killed him!

ROXY: She tempted him to her, and ... oh ... (*She clutches her chest.*) ... stopped his heart.

> *Spontaneously,* DARKLY *kneels at* ROXY's *feet.*

DARKLY: It takes a witch to do that!

ROXY: You took the words from my mouth ... (*Pause.*) But killing my husband was not enough for her. After that ... she put her spell on my son.

> ROXY *touches the boy in the photograph.* DARKLY *looks at the photograph.*

ROXY: My beautiful ... *silent* son.

> DARKLY *stares at photograph closely, then up at* ROXY. *Something is dawning on him ...*

DARKLY: Silent?

ROXY *nods, waiting.*

DARKLY: ... Clay? Your son is Clay?

ROXY (*nodding*): He can't resist her! It's not his fault. She's turned him against his own mother. But he's helpless.

DARKLY: Helpless ... yes!

ROXY: But he can never be happy with her. Never! And you know why?

DARKLY: Why?

ROXY: Because she can never have children. She told me that when I was nursing her. She's barren. She committed sins –

DARKLY: God has cursed her!

ROXY: I like you, boy.

ROXY *strokes* DARKLY's *hair. Slowly,* DARKLY *brings his head onto her lap.* ROXY *continues stroking his hair.*

DARKLY: Was it you ... who shot at the house?

ROXY: It was.

DARKLY: What you go and do a thing like that for?

ROXY: To remind her I'm still here. Watching. And waiting ... Waiting for her to be punished!

EXT. CALLIE'S HOMESTEAD. DAY

CALLIE *is fixing something on the electric generator beside the house. It sparks ominously and she curses. Wiping her hands on some cloth, she steps back, and into* DARKLY –

DARKLY: You ruined a family!

CALLIE: Lee! ... You made me jump! What? I ...

DARKLY: You ruined a family.

CALLIE: You've been to see her again.

DARKLY: Yes.

CALLIE: I told you not to. You don't understand anything, Lee.

128

DARKLY: You killed her husband!

CALLIE: Oh, Lee ...

DARKLY: They helped you. Brought y ... you in here. And you k ... killed her husband. Then put a spell on her son –

CALLIE: Keep your voice down! Clay'll hear you.

DARKLY: I d ... don't care.

CALLIE: Well, I care –

DARKLY: Witch!

CALLIE: What!

DARKLY: Witch!

CALLIE: That's what *she* says.

DARKLY: I'm saying it too! Witch! Witch!

The generator sparks violently again.

CALLIE: Listen, Lee! Listen! It's not like she says it was. No, listen! Roxy has already turned a whole town against me. Spreading lies, rumours: I killed her husband, bewitched Clay, threw her out of her own house. But, Lee, it's not true. You must believe me it's *not* the truth.

DARKLY is faltering know. Half of him wants so much to believe her.

DARKLY: But ...

CALLIE: Clay's Daddy tried to rape me. (*Pause.*) He died while doing it. And that's the truth ...

CALLIE is near tears now.

CALLIE: I haven't done anything wrong, Lee. Please ... You must believe me.

DARKLY is affected by CALLIE's distress.

DARKLY: I ... I ...

CALLIE: I just loved Clay, Lee. That's all I did. Please believe me. I'm not a ... a witch.

DARKLY: I'm sorry ...

CALLIE: I know, I know.

DARKLY: It's just that ... well, M ... Ma and Pa always
   said –
CALLIE: Forget your Ma and Pa.
DARKLY: But I c ... can't.
CALLIE: You're going to have to!
   DARKLY *stares at* CALLIE, *tears in his eyes.*
DARKLY: Oh, Callie.
CALLIE: It'll be alright, Lee. I promise.

INT. CALLIE'S HOMESTEAD, MAIN ROOM. NIGHT
CALLIE, CLAY *and* DARKLY *have just finished dinner.*
CALLIE *and* CLAY *are on sofa.* CLAY *fiddling with radio.*
Static fills air. No station yet.
   DARKLY *is clearing the table.* CALLIE *glances at* DARKLY
and, unseen by CLAY, *silently mouths ...*

CALLIE: You okay?
   DARKLY *nods.* CALLIE *embraces* CLAY.
CALLIE (*out loud now*): We're going to make this work here.
   I know we are. The three of us together like a family.
   Then ... The radio comes on. A song is on the radio. It's a
   dark, haunting love song called 'Look What You've Done
   (To My Skin)'.
      CLAY *looks at* CALLIE *triumphantly: Cluck, whistle.*
   CALLIE *kisses him.*
CALLIE (*at* DARKLY): I told you Clay was the only one who
   could get a song from the radio.
   CALLIE *and* CLAY *start to dance: whistle.* DARKLY
   watches ...
SONG (*on soundtrack*):

      I'm feeling lost
      And a little bit scared.
      I'm on a journey
      And I wasn't prepared.
130

The tell me it's risky.
I might not return.
Sometimes I'm freezing.
Sometimes I burn.

DARKLY's *stare is becoming more confused: half hopeless, half hostile. But* CALLIE *and* CLAY *are too engulfed in each other to notice. They just dance.*
Stare ...
Dance ...
Stare ...
DARKLY *storms out of the house.*

EXT. CALLIE'S HOMESTEAD. NIGHT
DARKLY *is walking away from the house. His face is hard, jaws clenched. There is something determined about him.*
The song continues on soundtrack ...

SONG:

This journey is changing me,
But what can I do?
It's a journey
I've got to make
A journey I've got to take.

INT. THE BARN, WORK AREA. NIGHT
DARKLY *goes straight to a corner. He starts searching for something. His search is frantic, yet determined. Several things are discarded, strewn across the barn. They clatter violently.*
DARKLY *knows exactly what he's looking for. Then he finds it! Barbed wire!*

132

SONG (*continued*):

> Look what you've done to my skin.
> Look what you've done to my heart.
> But I won't be scared.
> I'll see it through.
> This journey might
> Haunt me and hurt me.
> This journey is called loving you.

INT. THE BARN, LOFT. NIGHT
DARKLY's *eyes are fixed straight ahead, glazed, transfixed.*
DARKLY *unbuttons his shirt cuff buttons. Then the rest of the
buttons. He removes his shirt. Stripped to the waist, he turns to
look at the barbed wire ... He picks the wire up. Starts to
unravel it.*

SONG (*continued*):

> This feeling is scarey
> Like sparks on the skin.
> Oh, how it excites me.
> As thrilling as sin.

> I pray for forgiveness
> If this feeling is wrong.
> But while I'm praying
> Let the feeling go on.

> This journey is changing me.
> But what can I do?
> It's a journey
> I've got to make.
> A journey I've got to take.

*Then, slowly almost ritualistically, he begins wrapping the
barbed wire round his torso. The barbed wire digs into his
flesh.* DARKLY *winces, whimpers in agony. But, there's an*

ecstasy to it, too. *A pain he has to suffer. A pain to block another pain ...*

SONG (*continued*):

> Look what you've done to my skin.
> Look what you've done to my heart.
> But I won't be scared.
> I'll see it through.
> And though it might
> Hurt me and hurt me,
> This journey is called loving you.

Tenth Day

EXT. SKY. DAY
The sun is a blazing orb. We hear the distant sound of hammering ...
> *Hammering ... Hammering ...*

EXT. THE BARN. DAY
The sun blazes down on the barn.
> *Hammering ... Hammering ...*

INT. THE BARN, MAIN AREA. DAY
DARKLY *is armed with hammer and chisel. It is this hammering we've been hearing. There is stiffness about* DARKLY *now. The barbed wire is under his shirt, inhibiting his movements. And his emotions! His face is an expressionless mask, eyes glazed.*
> *Hammering ... Hammering ...*

CLAY *is working nearby, watching, concerned. He goes over to* DARKLY *and goes to touch his forehead.* DARKLY *flinches away.*

134

DARKLY: No, I'm not sick.

> *Hammering ...*

> > CLAY *resumes his work for a while. Then, still*
> > *concerned, returns.*

DARKLY: I ... have a pain in my ... h ... heart.

> *Hammering ...*

> > *Once more* CLAY *resumes work. But, once more, concern*
> > *gets the better of him. He returns.*

DARKLY: I'm missing my Ma and Pa. That's all, just
missing my Ma and my Pa.

> *Hammering ...*

> > CLAY *nods in understanding. He goes to embrace*
> > DARKLY. DARKLY *pulls away.*

DARKLY: Don't!

> *Hammering!*

> > *Hammering!*

> > > *Hammering!*

EXT. CALLIE'S HOMESTEAD. NIGHT
The homestead is bathed in moonlight.

> *Trees gigantic, threatening.*

> *Insects ...*

INT. CALLIE'S HOMESTEAD, KITCHEN. NIGHT
CALLIE, CLAY *and* DARKLY *are sitting round the table.*
CALLIE *and* CLAY *are eating.* DARKLY *stares ahead, he*
doesn't eat. His forehead is covered with perspiration now.

CALLIE: What's wrong?

DARKLY: Nothing.

CALLIE: Not hungry?

DARKLY: No.

CALLIE: Are you feeling sick?

DARKLY: No. Why does everyone think I'm sick around
here?

Abruptly, DARKLY *leaves ...*

EXT. CALLIE'S HOMESTEAD. NIGHT

DARKLY *exits.* CALLIE *follows him, concerned.*

CALLIE: Lee!

DARKLY *stops but does not turn round.*

CALLIE: Can I get you anything?

DARKLY: No.

CALLIE: Can I do anything?

DARKLY: I'm just trying to sort something out and when
I've sorted it out I'll be alright again.

CALLIE: But can I help?

CALLIE *approaches.* DARKLY *turns to face her.* CALLIE
stops dead in her tracks when she sees his face.

CALLIE: Why are you looking at me that way?

DARKLY *stares.*

A pause.

CALLIE: Listen, perhaps you should –

DARKLY: Do you want me to leave?

CALLIE: No. That's the last thing I want.

DARKLY *stares.*

CALLIE: You're scaring me ...

DARKLY *stares.*

CALLIE: Clay has a really bad temper. If he suspects that
you're –

DARKLY: What?

CALLIE: ... Nothing.

DARKLY: Say it!

CALLIE: ... Nothing.

DARKLY: What?

DARKLY *takes a step towards her.*

136

CALLIE: No! Don't!

> *The door to the house opens.* CLAY *walks on to the porch.*

CALLIE: It's alright, Clay.

> CLAY *looks at them both, waiting.*

CALLIE: Everything's alright. (*To* DARKLY.) See you in the morning. Lee.

> CALLIE *goes to* CLAY. *She kisses him and they go into the house.* DARKLY *walks angrily away from the house.*

DARKLY (*under his breath*): Witch! Witch! Witch!

EXT. THE FOREST. NIGHT

DARKLY *is marching through the forest. A storm is in full force.*

> *Lightning flashes.*
> *Thunder roars.*
> *Branches lash at him ...*
> *Rain whips at him.*
> DARKLY *begins running ...*
> *Lightning.*
> *Thunder.*
> *Rain.*
> *Running ...*
> *Running ...*
> *Running ...*

Eleventh Day

EXT. CLIFF TOP. DAY

DARKLY *is asleep on the edge of the cliff. Far below, and stretching as far as the eye can see, is the forest. For a moment* DARKLY *is still. Then ... His hand starts to twitch. It's covered with ants. We see* DARKLY's *face. His face is covered in ants as well. His face starts to twitch.*

DARKLY's *twitching wakes him up. He sees the ants and jumps to his feet.*

DARKLY: Ahhh ... No! No!
  He frantically brushes the insects from him ...

EXT. THE FOREST. DAY
DARKLY *is staggering along, still brushing the ants from him, panting. The sun is bright and dazzling.*
  Insects ...
  Birds ...
  Panting ...

EXT. THE FOREST, OUTSIDE ROXY'S MOBILE HOME. DAY
DARKLY *opens the mobile home's door. He goes inside ...*

INT. ROXY'S MOBILE HOME. DAY
DARKLY *enters and looks at ...* ROXY *is sitting on the floor. She is weeping. On her lap is* DOG *– dead. It's limply sprawled across her legs.*

DARKLY: What happened?
ROXY: Dead ... dead and gone ... (*Gazes at* DARKLY, *tears in her eyes.*) I'm all alone now. Nothing to love ... Nothing to live for.
  DARKLY *is just staring ...*
ROXY: Gotta say goodbye to her. She won't go to heaven if I don't say goodbye.
DARKLY: Animals don't go to heaven.
ROXY: Oh, they do. You just gotta know how to say goodbye right ... That's what I believe. Come on ... Come on ...
  138

EXT. THE FOREST. DAY
ROXY *and* DARKLY *are walking through the forest.* DARKLY
is holding the dead dog.

ROXY: Dead dog.
DARKLY: Dead dog.
ROXY: Say goodbye.
DARKLY: Goodbye.
ROXY: Go to heaven.
DARKLY: Heaven.
  They continue walking towards ...

EXT. FOREST, NEAR LAKE. DAY
ROXY *comes to a halt, looking at the lake. On the bank is a
giant silver shoe.* DARKLY *stands behind her, still holding the*
DOG.

ROXY (*indicating shoe*): Where that come from ... ? Well, I
  don't know where it come from but if I get hold of it I
  do know where it's going ...
  She walks towards silver shoe. DARKLY *follows.*

EXT. THE FOREST, RIVER BANK. DAY
ROXY *is paddling in the water. Her black dress has risen and
floats around her. In front of her, floating on the surface of the
river, is the large, silver shoe. In the shoe we see the dead* DOG.
The DOG *is in a nest of twigs.*

  DARKLY *stands on the bank, watching.* ROXY *bends forward
and kisses the* DOG.

ROXY: Go to heaven ...
  *Then she strikes a match and sets fire to the twigs. She
  pushes the shoe out into the current of the river. The
  current carries it away ...*

139

Flames rise up from the shoe ... Sparks fly up.

There is a haunting beauty to the image: the burning dog, the firelight reflected in the silver of the shoe and in the water ...

DARKLY *watches, fascinated. The total madness of the image seems to touch some rising madness in him ...*

Fire!

Burning Dog!

Silver!

Fire!

Burning ... burning ... burning ...

EXT. THE FOREST. DAY

DARKLY *is stumbling through the forest.*

EXT. FOREST, BY BIG TREE. DAY

DARKLY *stumbles into shot and falls to his knees. Then he hears something ...*

MA´S VOICE (*off screen*): Darkly!

PA´S VOICE (*off screen*): Darkly!

DARKLY *looks all around.*

DARKLY: Pa? Ma? Is that you? Where are you?

MA/PA (*off screen*): We're here ... up here, Darkly.

DARKLY *begins to look up. The camera follows his gaze.*

There, in the branches of the tree above, are the grotesque bodies of DARKLY's MA *and* PA. *They're dressed exactly as we've been seeing them in the photograph. Only now their faces are deathly white ...*

Their eyes are glazed. Their clothes are scorched. And there are bullet holes in their bodies and faces. Bullet holes rimmed with dried blood.

PA: Don't be scared, son. We're here to help you. Right, Ma?

140

MA: Right, Pa.

PA: We're here to tell you what you're to do.

    DARKLY *begins backing away.*

PA: You've got the Lord's work to do.

MA: The Lord's work!

    DARKLY *runs ... But his parents' voices pursue him ...*

PA: The Lord's work!

MA: The Lord's work!

PA: The Lord's work!

MA: The Lord's work!

PA: The Lord's work!

EXT. THE FOREST. DAY

DARKLY *rushes into shot. He falls to his knees. He madly stares all around him. Gradually, he gets his breath back. He calms down a little. Then ...*

   A determined look comes into his eyes. He knows what to do next. He knows where to go ... He jumps up and runs towards ...

EXT. CALLIE'S HOMESTEAD. DAY

DARKLY *rushes up to the house. He stands outside and shrieks.*

DARKLY: Callie!

INT. CALLIE'S HOMESTEAD, KITCHEN. DAY

CALLIE *is asleep on the sofa.*

EXT. CALLIE'S HOMESTEAD. DAY

DARKLY *shrieks again ...*

DARKLY: Callie!

INT. THE BARN, WORK AREA. DAY
CLAY *is busy working. He hears* DARKLY*'s call, looks up ...*

EXT. CALLIE'S HOMESTEAD. DAY
DARKLY *shrieks again ...*

DARKLY: Callie!

INT. CALLIE'S HOMESTEAD, KITCHEN. DAY
CALLIE *wakes.*

CALLIE: Lee?
 She gets up ...

INT. THE BARN, WORK AREA. DAY
CLAY *leaves barn ...*

EXT. CALLIE'S HOMESTEAD. DAY
CALLIE *comes out of the house and sees* DARKLY.

CALLIE: Where have you been? I've been worried sick about
 you – (*Notices the state he's in.*) Jesus! What happened to
 you?
 DARKLY *just stares.* CALLIE *goes to touch him.* DARKLY
 pulls away ... CLAY *rushes over to them.*
CALLIE: What happened?
 CLAY *sees the state of* DARKLY, *goes to help.* DARKLY
 pushes him away. CLAY *begins to get angry.*
CALLIE: Clay! It's alright.
 DARKLY *is building himself up into an hysterical state.*
 Suddenly, DARKLY *makes a lunge for* CALLIE. CLAY
 pushes him away. DARKLY *falls back.*

142

CALLIE: Oh, no, don't! Don't hurt him, Clay! Lee, just go.
Leave! Please.

DARKLY *rushes forward again. Another struggle ensues
between* CLAY *and* DARKLY. CLAY *pushes* DARKLY.
DARKLY *falls to the ground.*

CALLIE (*sobbing*): No! No! Oh, my God! No!

CALLIE *tries to pull* CLAY *off* DARKLY ...

CALLIE: Clay! Don't! Lee! Keep calm. Lee! Stop it! Stop it!

DARKLY *jumps to his feet and lunges at* CLAY *again.*

CALLIE: Oh, my God!

CALLIE *is clutching at* DARKLY's *shirt.* CLAY *punches*
DARKLY. DARKLY *falls to the ground – his shirt ripping.
The barbed wire is revealed, still wrapped round him.
And his chest: Blood covered, cut, bruised, savaged.*

CALLIE: Oh, my God!

CALLIE *and* CLAY *stare at* DARKLY. DARKLY *glares up
at them.*

CALLIE: Take your things and go!

DARKLY *hesitates.*

CALLIE: You've got to, Lee. You've got no choice.

CLAY *kicks at* DARKLY.

CALLIE: Don't, Clay! Leave him. He's going! Look! He's
going!

DARKLY *struggles to his feet, then goes to the barn ...*

INT. THE BARN, LOFT AREA. DAY
DARKLY *grabs his tin box.*

EXT. CALLIE'S HOMESTEAD. DAY
DARKLY *leaves the barn, holding tin box.* CALLIE *and* CLAY
are sitting on the porch. CLAY *has his arms around* CALLIE.
Slowly, DARKLY *points at* CALLIE.

DARKLY: Time for my walk in the dark.

CALLIE (*sobbing*): No!

> CLAY *holds* CALLIE *tighter, glaring at* DARKLY.
> DARKLY *walks into the forest* ...

INT. THE CAVE. DAY

DARKLY *enters cave, exhausted. He collapses, then looks up at the cave wall. He sees the red hand print. It looks quite beautiful, magical* ...

INT. CALLIE'S HOMESTEAD, KITCHEN. EARLY EVENING

CALLIE *and* CLAY *are sitting on the sofa.* CLAY *is drinking beer.* CALLIE *still looks distressed.* JUDE *is facing them.*

JUDE: Gone? Gone where?

CALLIE: I don't know. He just went ...

> JUDE *stares, wanting more. Slight pause.*

CALLIE: I told him to go.

JUDE: Why?

> CALLIE *shakes her head, unable to answer.* CLAY *grunts irritably.*

JUDE: He was just a kid, for God's sake! He was ill.

CALLIE: I know, I know.

JUDE: Have you any idea where he could be?

> CALLIE *glances nervously at* CLAY, *then shakes her head.*

JUDE: Come on, Callie. He wouldn't just go. He was my friend. Besides he had nothing. He had nowhere to go.

> CLAY *is getting increasingly irritated by* JUDE's *questions.*
> *Cluck! Cluck! Whistle!*

CALLIE: Just go on out to work. I'm fine. Go on.

> CLAY *finishes his beer and gets up. He takes rifle from wall and loads it.*

CALLIE: Clay! Leave the rifle here!

> CLAY *hands rifle to* CALLIE, *then leaves.*

145

CALLIE: I didn't want to say anything in front of Clay. If he knows where he can find him I think he'll kill him.

JUDE: You know where he is?

CALLIE *stares intently at* JUDE.

CALLIE: Is it my fault?

JUDE *cannot answer.*

A beat.

CALLIE: Is it something I did?

Again JUDE *cannot answer. All he can say is ...*

JUDE: Callie, where is he?

CALLIE: Well ... you can try somewhere. He might just be there.

JUDE: Where?

CALLIE (*softly*): My favourite place in the whole world.

EXT. THE FOREST, PATH TO CAVE. EVENING
JUDE *approaches the cave, looking all round.*

JUDE: Lee? You up here? Lee?

INT. CAVE. EVENING
In his delirium, DARKLY *responds to* JUDE *calling. He moans ...*

EXT. THE FOREST, OUTSIDE CAVE. EVENING
JUDE *hears moan and ...*

JUDE: Lee!

INT. THE CAVE. EVENING
JUDE *rushes into cave. He sees* DARKLY *and goes to him.*

146

JUDE: Oh, Jesus Christ! ... What are you doing here? What's going on?

DARKLY (*faintly*): Leave ... me ... alone ...

JUDE: Leave you?

DARKLY: Just go! Just leave me alone.

> JUDE *goes to feel* DARKLY'S *forehead.* DARKLY *backs away.*

DARKLY: No!

JUDE: Oh, hell, you're coming with me. Come on.

DARKLY: No! No! Not yet.

JUDE: Listen! You remember what I said. About me running away. I'm doing it. Tomorrow night. I'm taking the truck and I'm gone. And you're coming with me. The two of us. We're getting out of this forest once and for all.

DARKLY: No!

JUDE: Alright! Alright!

> *A beat.*

DARKLY: Tomorrow night.

JUDE: Alright! I'll come back for you. Here. Tomorrow night.

DARKLY: ... Yes.

JUDE: You'll hang on till then. Okay?

DARKLY: Okay.

> JUDE *hesitates for a moment, then stands and leaves.* DARKLY *clutches the tin box tighter.*

EXT. THE FOREST, ROXY'S MOBILE HOME. NIGHT
Moonlight gleams on silver.

INT. ROXY'S MOBILE HOME. NIGHT
ROXY *sits on edge of bed. She's been drinking. She's just finishing cleaning her rifle. She reaches out ... Gets a bullet. She loads rifle. She puts rifle into mouth ... And pulls trigger.*

147

INT. THE CAVE. NIGHT
The shot wakes DARKLY. *He sits up in a cold sweat.*

DARKLY: Roxy!

Twelfth Day

EXT. THE FOREST. DAY
DARKLY *is walking relentlessly. His skin is grimy. Clothes filthy. Eyes staring ahead ...*

EXT. THE FOREST, PATH TO ROXY'S SILVER BULLET. DAY
DARKLY *strides up to the mobile home. He opens the door and ...*

INT. ROXY'S MOBILE HOME. DAY
DARKLY *enters. He looks round and sees* ROXY *on her bed. The back of her head is missing. Blood over bed and wall. The rifle is laying at her feet.*
  DARKLY *collapses and starts weeping. Then ...*

MA (*off screen*): Darkly ... Darkly, don't upset yourself, son.
   DARKLY *looks round to see ... His* MA *and* PA *are sitting nearby.*
PA: Good morning, son.
MA: Did you see what she did?
PA: A terrible sin.
MA: Don't think I've ever known a forest with more sin, have you, Pa?
PA: Don't think I have, Ma.
DARKLY: Oh, Ma! Pa! I'm sorry I ran away the other day. I was very scared.
PA: Don't mention it, son.

149

MA: You been eating properly?

DARKLY: Yes, ma'am.

PA: And saying your prayers?

DARKLY: Yes, sir.

MA: Every night?

DARKLY: Well ...

PA: Don't lie to us, son.

DARKLY: Well, almost every night, it's just that ... I do when I can.

PA: You know you should say them every night, son. Praise the Lord for all his merciful blessings.

DARKLY: I've tried. It's just that it's very difficult here. And ... there's a lot that I don't understand.

PA: Oh, I know, son. But you're here for a reason. Hallelujah!

MA: Hallelujah!

DARKLY: I am?

PA: Course you are, son. Shall we tell him, Ma?

MA: I think so, Pa.

PA: Now listen, son. There was once a happy family in this forest. Clay, his poor mother here, and her husband. A good family. And then – why then a witch came upon them and spoiled their happiness forever.

DARKLY: Pa?

PA: Yes, son?

DARKLY: Callie said that ... that it was Clay's father who tried to ... to attack her ... and that –

PA: And you believe that, son? You believe her lies? I don't think we do. Do we, Ma?

MA: Of course not, Pa.

PA: It was her! All her! Putting a spell on men! Don't tell me you can't feel it yourself, son? Look at you! Look at what she's done to you! She's cursed you, son! But it wasn't your fault. It's hers! You're helpless in the spell of a witch.

150

DARKLY: You know ... I am.

PA: But you've got to fight back, son. That's the reason you're here. God has tested you and you've got to prove to him you've passed the test.

DARKLY: Pa?

PA: You got to purify the forest. You know the way it is, son – the word of our Lord. When someone sins, try to forgive them. And if you can't ... well ... kill them.

MA: No faith without blood. Right, Pa?

A beat.

PA (*at* DARKLY): You know what you've got to do?

DARKLY *nods.*

MA: Hallelujah!

PA: Hallelujah!

DARKLY: Hallelujah!

Final Night

INT. THE CAVE. NIGHT

DARKLY *is sitting in front of a small fire. He is gazing into the flames.*

The firelight gives DARKLY *a demonic quality. Beside* DARKLY *is the tin box. And a can of red paint. It's the red paint he'd been painting the cradle with earlier.*

EXT. CALLIE'S HOMESTEAD, THE PORCH. NIGHT

CLAY *comes out of the house and sits on the porch. He is drinking a bottle of beer, relaxing.*

INT. CAVE. NIGHT

DARKLY *begins removing the bandage from his hand.*

EXT. CALLIE'S HOMESTEAD, PORCH. NIGHT
CLAY *lights a cigarette*.

INT. CAVE. NIGHT
DARKLY *finishing unbandaging hand*.

EXT. CALLIE'S HOMESTEAD, PORCH. NIGHT
CLAY *begins smoking cigarette*.

INT. CAVE. NIGHT
DARKLY *throws bandage into fire*.

EXT. CALLIE'S HOMESTEAD, PORCH. NIGHT
CLAY *drinks beer*.

INT. CAVE. NIGHT
DARKLY *removes jacket. He throws it on the fire*.

EXT. CALLIE'S HOMESTEAD, PORCH. NIGHT
CALLIE *comes out of house. She sits next to* CLAY *on the porch*.

INT. CAVE. NIGHT
DARKLY *unbuttons shirt*.

EXT. CALLIE'S HOMESTEAD, PORCH. NIGHT
CALLIE *takes sip from* CLAY*'s beer bottle*.

153

INT. CAVE. NIGHT
DARKLY *removes shirt. He throws it on fire. His torso is horrifically scarred by the barbed wire, which is still wrapped barbarically round him.*

EXT. CALLIE'S HOMESTEAD, PORCH. NIGHT
CALLIE *and* CLAY *start kissing.*

INT. CAVE. NIGHT
DARKLY*'s jacket burns.*

EXT. CALLIE'S HOMESTEAD, PORCH. NIGHT
CALLIE *and* CLAY*'s kissing becomes more intense.*

INT. CAVE. NIGHT
The jacket burns.

EXT. CALLIE'S HOMESTEAD, PORCH. NIGHT
Kissing.

INT. CAVE. NIGHT
DARKLY *picks up the can of red paint. He unscrews the cap.*

EXT. CALLIE'S HOMESTEAD, PORCH. NIGHT
Kissing.

INT. CAVE. NIGHT
DARKLY *pours red paint into one of his hands.*

EXT. CALLIE'S HOMESTEAD, PORCH. NIGHT
Kissing.

INT. CAVE. NIGHT
DARKLY*'s hand has turned red.*

EXT. CALLIE'S HOMESTEAD, PORCH. NIGHT
CALLIE *and* CLAY *stand, still kissing.* CLAY *picks* CALLIE *up.*

INT. CAVE. NIGHT
DARKLY *rubs paint on his right arm.*

EXT. CALLIE'S HOMESTEAD, PORCH. NIGHT
CLAY *takes* CALLIE *over to door into house.*

INT. CAVE. NIGHT
DARKLY *begins to rub paint over his left arm.*

EXT. CALLIE'S HOMESTEAD, PORCH. NIGHT
CALLIE *and* CLAY*, their passion rising, go into the house.*

INT. CAVE. NIGHT
DARKLY *completes rubbing paint over his left arm.*

INT. CALLIE'S HOMESTEAD, HALLWAY. NIGHT
CLAY *carries* CALLIE *into the house. Her legs are wrapped around him. They are kissing passionately.*

INT. CAVE. NIGHT
Red paint splashes on the ground.

INT. CALLIE'S HOMESTEAD, HALLWAY. NIGHT
CALLIE *and* CLAY *start undoing each other's clothes.*

INT. CAVE. NIGHT
DARKLY *begins to rub red paint across his neck.*

INT. CALLIE'S HOMESTEAD, HALLWAY. NIGHT
CLAY *removes* CALLIE*'s top.*

INT. CAVE. NIGHT
DARKLY *completes spreading red paint across his neck.*

INT. CALLIE'S HOMESTEAD, HALLWAY. NIGHT
CALLIE*'s top falls to the floor.*

INT. CAVE. NIGHT
Red paint splashes in tin box.
   Over the Bible.
   Over the photos of MA *and* PA*.*
   Over the apple core.
   Over the barbed wire bird.

INT. CALLIE'S HOMESTEAD, HALLWAY. NIGHT
CALLIE *starts undoing* CLAY*'s shirt.*

INT. CAVE. NIGHT
DARKLY *rubs paint across right side of his face.*

INT. CALLIE'S HOMESTEAD, HALLWAY. NIGHT
CALLIE *reaches between* CLAY's *legs.*

INT. CAVE. NIGHT
DARKLY *rubs paint across the left side of his face.*

INT. CALLIE'S HOMESTEAD, HALLWAY. NIGHT
CALLIE *pushes* CLAY *playfully away from her. Their love-making has become more violent.*

EXT. CAVE. NIGHT
DARKLY *completes rubbing paint over his face.*

INT. CALLIE'S HOMESTEAD, HALLWAY. NIGHT
CALLIE *rips* CLAY's *shirt off.* CLAY *rips* CALLIE's *dress off.*

EXT. CAVE. NIGHT
DARKLY *gets some soot from fire. He begins to darken the area round his eyes.*

INT. CALLIE'S HOMESTEAD, HALLWAY. NIGHT
CLAY *pushes* CALLIE *against the wall. He feels between her legs. They are both extremely aroused.*

INT. CAVE. NIGHT
DARKLY *stares into camera. He is covered in red paint. Eyes dark. A red demon . . .*

INT. CALLIE'S HOMESTEAD, HALLWAY/KITCHEN. NIGHT
CLAY *carries* CALLIE *over to the kitchen table . . .*

INT. CAVE. NIGHT
DARKLY *puts his hand on the red hand print on the cave
wall . . .*

INT. CALLIE'S HOMESTEAD, KITCHEN. NIGHT
CLAY *and* CALLIE *make love on the kitchen table . . .*

INT. CAVE. NIGHT
DARKLY *picks up large chisel tool. It glints threateningly in the
firelight . . .*

INT. CALLIE'S HOMESTEAD, KITCHEN. NIGHT
CLAY *and* CALLIE *continue making love . . .*

INT. CAVE. NIGHT
DARKLY *leaves cave . . .*

INT. CALLIE'S HOMESTEAD, KITCHEN. NIGHT
CLAY *and* CALLIE *make love . . .*

EXT. FOREST. NIGHT
DARKLY *walks through the forest . . .*

INT. CALLIE'S HOMESTEAD, KITCHEN. NIGHT
CLAY *and* CALLIE *make love . . .*

EXT. FOREST, NEAR CAVE. NIGHT
JUDE *pulls up in his truck. He gets out, lights a flash light.
Then he looks up to the cave entrance . . .*

JUDE (*calling*): Lee? You ready, partner?

INT. CALLIE'S HOMESTEAD, KITCHEN. NIGHT
CALLIE *and* CLAY *go to the sofa* ...

EXT. CALLIE'S HOMESTEAD. NIGHT
DARKLY *approaches the house* ...

INT. CAVE. NIGHT
JUDE *enters the cave* ...

JUDE (*calling*): Lee?

EXT. CALLIE'S HOMESTEAD, PORCH. NIGHT
DARKLY *steps up onto the porch. He goes to the window and
looks through. He sees* ...

INT. CALLIE'S HOMESTEAD, KITCHEN. NIGHT
CLAY *and* CALLIE *making love* ...

INT. CAVE. NIGHT
JUDE *is looking round the cave. He sees the red paint* ...

EXT. CALLIE'S HOMESTEAD, PORCH. NIGHT
DARKLY *watches* CLAY *and* CALLIE ...

INT. CAVE. NIGHT
JUDE *looks at the fire box. The Bible. The barbed wire object.
Then he sees the red hand print on the wall* ...

INT. CALLIE'S HOMESTEAD, KITCHEN. NIGHT
CALLIE *sees* DARKLY *looking through the window. She
screams...*

INT. CAVE. NIGHT
JUDE *has put the pieces together.*

JUDE: Callie!
   He runs from the cave ...

INT. CALLIE'S HOMESTEAD, KITCHEN/HALLWAY. NIGHT
DARKLY *smashes through the window! Glass shatters every-
where!*
   *As he bursts into the house, the chisel tool smashes into a
lamp. It explodes! The dodgy electrics start to crackle and fizz.
They ignite everywhere, setting fire to the house.*
   DARKLY *stares at* CLAY *and* CALLIE.

DARKLY: I am your punishment!
   DARKLY *lunges at them.* CALLIE *flees one way.* CLAY *the
   other.*
      More electrics explode!
      DARKLY *hits* CLAY.
CALLIE: For the love of God!
DARKLY: Precisely!
   DARKLY *lunges at* CALLIE *with the weapon. She
   screams, hides behind the table. The weapon crashes into
   the table.*
      CLAY *reaches for the rifle and aims it at* DARKLY.
      DARKLY *hears* CLAY. *He turns and knocks rifle from*
   CLAY's *hand.*
CALLIE: Lee! Stop it! Stop it!
      CALLIE *jumps on* DARKLY's *back.* DARKLY *flings her*

aside, then stabs at CLAY. *The weapon pierces* CLAY's
shoulder ...

EXT. THE FOREST. NIGHT
JUDE *is running frantically ...*

INT. CALLIE'S HOMESTEAD, KITCHEN/HALLWAY. NIGHT
DARKLY *punches* CLAY. CLAY *falls to the floor.* DARKLY
raises weapon to kill him.

   Suddenly, CALLIE *lunges at* DARKLY *with a small kitchen
knife. She stabs him in the shoulder.* DARKLY *yells out, then
grabs* CALLIE *round the neck. He pushes her savagely to the
ground.* CLAY *picks up the rifle again. He cocks the trigger.*
DARKLY *hears this, turns on* CLAY, *and pushes him violently
out of the house ...*

EXT. CALLIE'S HOMESTEAD. NIGHT
CLAY *shoots out of the house. He crashes painfully to the
ground ...*

INT. CALLIE'S HOMESTEAD, HALLWAY. NIGHT
DARKLY *approaches* CALLIE, *raising the weapon threateningly.* CALLIE *backs away. Explosions are happening
everywhere now. Fire filling the house ...*

INT. CALLIE'S HOMESTEAD, THE STAIRS. NIGHT
CALLIE *backs up the stairs.* DARKLY *pursues her.*
   Explosions!
   Fire!

EXT. THE FOREST. NIGHT
JUDE *is running . . .*

EXT. CALLIE'S HOMESTEAD. NIGHT
CLAY *tries to get up. He gasps painfully, collapses. His leg is broken . . .*

INT. CALLIE'S HOMESTEAD, HALLWAY TO BEDROOM. NIGHT
CALLIE *backs away from* DARKLY. *He pursues her. The electrics are exploding alongside* DARKLY. *As if his mere presence causes them.*
Fire!
Fire!

EXT. CALLIE'S HOMESTEAD. NIGHT
CLAY *starts to crawl towards the house . . .*

INT. CALLIE'S HOMESTEAD, BEDROOM. NIGHT
CALLIE *backs into the bedroom.* DARKLY *stands in the doorway.* CALLIE *is crying.*
DARKLY *hits the light switch by the door with his weapon. The light switch explodes! The doorway bursts into fire.* DARKLY *lets out a deafening shriek . . .*

EXT. CALLIE'S HOMESTEAD, MAIN HOUSE. NIGHT
A chain reaction of electrical explosions is set off. The wires connecting the main house to the barn, sparkle with fire . . .

EXT. CALLIE'S HOMESTEAD, THE BARN. NIGHT
The barn catches fire!

INT. THE BARN, LOFT. NIGHT
The loft catches fire! DARKLY's *bed ignites!*

EXT. CALLIE'S HOMESTEAD. NIGHT
The generator beside the house explodes. This makes —

INT. CALLIE'S HOMESTEAD, MAIN ROOM. NIGHT
— the wall cave in.

EXT. THE FOREST. NIGHT
JUDE *hears the explosions...*

EXT. CALLIE'S HOMESTEAD. NIGHT
CLAY *is still trying to get back in house...*

INT. CALLIE'S HOMESTEAD, BEDROOM. NIGHT
DARKLY *approaches* CALLIE. CALLIE *backs away, pressing tight against the wall, whimpering.*
  The room is blazing now. Everything is fire, fire, fire ...
  DARKLY *raises the weapon to kill her —*

CALLIE: I love you.
  DARKLY *freezes.*

EXT. CALLIE'S HOMESTEAD. NIGHT
CLAY *is crawling up the step to the porch.* JUDE *rushes up.*

JUDE: Clay! Where's Callie?
  CLAY *indicates inside the burning house.* JUDE *goes to rush inside —* CLAY *holds him back, indicates the rifle.* JUDE *must take the rifle.* JUDE *picks it up and —*

163

INT. CALLIE'S HOMESTEAD, HALLWAY. NIGHT
– *rushes into burning house. He shields his face against the flames. Then –*

INT. CALLIE'S HOMESTEAD, THE STAIRS. NIGHT
– JUDE *rushes up the burning stairs. Towards the bedroom where –*

INT. CALLIE'S HOMESTEAD, BEDROOM. NIGHT
DARKLY *is still staring at* CALLIE.

CALLIE: I love you, Darkly.
   Suddenly, JUDE *appears in the door. He aims the rifle.*
   CALLIE *glances at him.*
      JUDE *shoots the rifle.*
      Bang!
      The bullet goes through DARKLY's *heart. Blood sprays over* CALLIE's *face.* DARKLY *falls to the ground.*
      A beat.
      CALLIE *kneels beside* DARKLY. *Slowly,* JUDE *enters the room and kneels down.*
DARKLY (*softly*): Who will love me now?
   DARKLY *dies.*
      The room is rapidly turning into an inferno now.
      Fire ... fire ... fire ... fire ...
JUDE: He's dead, Callie.
CALLIE: No. No ...
   The fire in the room is raging now. Flames very close to them.
JUDE: Callie ...
CALLIE: I could have stopped him.
JUDE: We've got to go, Callie.
CALLIE: No ...
   164

JUDE: We've got to go!

> JUDE *pulls* CALLIE, *who is weeping, out of the inferno ...*

EXT. CALLIE'S HOMESTEAD. NIGHT
JUDE and CALLIE *rush out of the burning house. They pull* CLAY *away from the flames. Then, at a safe distance, they all look back as the house is engulfed by –*

> *Fire ...*
> *Fire ...*
> *Fire ...*
> *Fire ...*
> *Fire ...*

Next Day

EXT. CALLIE'S HOMESTEAD. DAY
Nothing left of the house. Just a scorched patch – like the terrain of another planet.

> CALLIE *is staring at the ruins.* CLAY *and* JUDE *are nearby.* CLAY's *leg is in a splint.*
> *A beat.*

JUDE: Callie?

> CALLIE *looks at* JUDE.

CALLIE: There's nothing left of him.

> CALLIE *continues looking at the ruins.*
> *Another beat.*
> *Then ...*

RINGMASTER (*off screen*): Hello?

> CALLIE *looks up and sees ... A group of people are approaching them. A* RINGMASTER, *his* WIFE *and their small child, an eight-year-old* BOY. *The boy is clutching a silver shoe. An* ELEPHANT *follows them, with its*

TRAINER.

The circus family come up to CALLIE.

RINGMASTER: My God! You folks had a tragedy!

CALLIE: ... Yes.

RINGMASTER: Same with us ... See, I run a circus. Few days ago the boat we were using to cross the river sank. We lost just about everything. Our giant silver shoe went floating off ... Now all we got left is this little model. It's my son's favourite thing.

CALLIE *looks at the* BOY. *The* BOY *smiles back.*

CALLIE: It's very beautiful.

The BOY *clutches the shoe tighter.*

RINGMASTER: By the way, this is my family.

RINGMASTER *indicates the others.* CALLIE *smiles at them.*

RINGMASTER: We've all been lost since the wreck. Funny ... I thought you could only go halfway into the forest ... And then you start making your way out.

CALLIE: No. It can go on forever sometimes.

RINGMASTER: Do you know the way out?

CALLIE: Yes.

EXT. CALLIE'S HOMESTEAD. DAY
A little later.

CLAY, *helped by* JUDE *and the* RINGMASTER, *is moving away from the house.* CALLIE, *alone, stares at the burnt remains.* JUDE *looks back* ...

JUDE: Callie! Come on:

The BOY *hears* JUDE *call. He sees* CALLIE *holding back and goes up to her.* BOY *gives* CALLIE *his silver shoe.*

CALLIE: This for me?

BOY *nods.*

166

CALLIE: Thank you.

    BOY *rejoins the others.*

    CALLIE *gives the ruined house one last look, then turns away. Clutching the shoe, she leaves the forest ...*
Cut to black.
Roll credits.

Song – Who Will Love Me Now?

    In the forest
    Is a monster
    It has done
    Terrible things
    So in the wood
    It's hiding
    And this is
    The song it sings

    Who will love me now?
    Who will ever love me?
    Who will say to me
    You are my desire
    I set you free

    Who will forgive
    And make me live again?
    Who will bring me back
    To the world again?

    In the forest
    Is a monster
    And it looks so
    Very much like me
    Will someone
    Hear me singing
    Please save me
    Please rescue me

Who will love me now?
Who will ever love me?
Who will say to me
You are my desire
I set you free

Who will love me now?
Who will ever love me?
Who will love me now?
Who will ever love me?

Methuen Modern Plays

include work by

Jean Anouilh
John Arden
Margaretta D'Arcy
Peter Barnes
Sebastian Barry
Brendan Behan
Edward Bond
Bertolt Brecht
Howard Brenton
Simon Burke
Jim Cartwright
Caryl Churchill
Noël Coward
Sarah Daniels
Nick Dear
Shelagh Delaney
David Edgar
Dario Fo
Michael Frayn
John Godber
Paul Godfrey
David Greig
John Guare
Peter Handke
Jonathan Harvey
Iain Heggie
Declan Hughes
Terry Johnson
Sarah Kane
Charlotte Keatley
Barrie Keeffe
Robert Lepage
Stephen Lowe

Doug Lucie
Martin McDonagh
John McGrath
David Mamet
Patrick Marber
Arthur Miller
Mtwa, Ngema & Simon
Tom Murphy
Phyllis Nagy
Peter Nichols
Joseph O'Connor
Joe Orton
Louise Page
Joe Penhall
Luigi Pirandello
Stephen Poliakoff
Franca Rame
Mark Ravenhill
Philip Ridley
Reginald Rose
David Rudkin
Willy Russell
Jean-Paul Sartre
Sam Shepard
Wole Soyinka
C. P. Taylor
Theatre de Complicite
Theatre Workshop
Sue Townsend
Judy Upton
Timberlake Wertenbaker
Victoria Wood

Methuen World Classics *and*
Methuen Contemporary Dramatists

Methuen Student Editions

new and forthcoming titles in the Methuen Film *series*

Persuasion
Nick Dear after Jane Austen

Beautiful Thing
Jonathan Harvey

The Crucible
Arthur Miller

The English Patient
Anthony Minghella

Twelfth Night
Trevor Nunn after Shakespeare

The Krays
Philip Ridley

The Reflecting Skin & The Passion of Darkly Noon
Philip Ridley